Big Data, Big Design

Why Designers Should Care About Artificial Intelligence

HELEN ARMSTRONG

WITH ILLUSTRATIONS BY KEETRA DEAN DIXON

Princeton Architectural Press, New York

Published by
Princeton Architectural Press
202 Warren Street
Hudson, New York 12534
www.papress.com

Book Designer: Helen Armstrong
Illustrator: Keetra Dean Dixon
Research Assistants: Isabel Bo-Linn and Eryn Pierce
Editors: Jennifer Thompson and Kristen Hewitt, Princeton Architectural Press
Typography: Chercán, designed by Francisco Gálvez in 2016

Library of Congress Cataloging-in-Publication Data
Names: Armstrong, Helen, 1971-author. | Dixon, Keetra Dean, illustrator.
Title: Big data, big design : why designers should care about AI / [edited by]
Helen Armstrong; with illustrations by Keetra Dean Dixon.
Description: First edition. | Hudson, New York : Princeton Architectural Press, 2021
Includes bibliographical references and index.
Summary: "Big Data. Big Design. (BDBD) demystifies machine learning (ML)
while inspiring designers to harness this technology and establish leadership
via thoughtful human-centered design"—Provided by publisher.
Identifiers: LCCN 2021006603 | ISBN 9781616899158 (paperback)
Subjects: LCSH: Product design—Data processing. | Design—Data processing.
Computer-aided design. | Designers—Interviews. | Artificial intelligence. | Big data.
Classification: LCC TS171.4 .B524 2021 | DDC 658.5/752—dc23
LC record available at https://lccn.loc.gov/2021006603

Helen Armstrong, a professor of graphic design at
North Carolina State University, focuses her research on
accessible design, digital rights, and machine learning.
Armstrong is the author of *Graphic Design Theory: Readings
from the Field* and *Digital Design Theory: Readings from
the Field*, and she is the coauthor of *Participate: Designing
with User-Generated Content.*

DESIGN BRIEFS—
essential texts on design

ALSO AVAILABLE IN THIS SERIES:

*Form + Code in Design, Art, and
Architecture,* Casey Reas, Chandler
McWilliams, LUST

*Introduction to Three-Dimensional
Design Principles, Processes, and
Projects,* Kimberly Elam

Thinking with Type, 2nd edition,
Ellen Lupton

Contents

Acknowledgments

My initial interest in machine learning (ML) sprang from my desire to use this technology to design individualized experiences for my special-needs kiddo. Technology has failed to meet the needs of a large swath of the population. ML can help provide access and meet those needs—or it can amplify marginalization. We stand before both possibilities.

Technology's failures stood out starkly during the Covid-19 pandemic, a period during which the bulk of this text took form. Special acknowledgment to all the parents who, like me, spent the pandemic running back and forth between their laptops and their kids' laptops—particularly the special needs parents who had to adapt everything on the fly so that their children might continue to learn.

I, myself, would not have survived without the support of my partner, Sean Krause, and the positive spirit and can-do attitude of my two children, Vivian and Tess. With their help, this book came to fruition. In addition, thank you to my wonderful colleagues at North Carolina State University for their continuous inspiration and support. Thank you Denise Gonzales-Crisp, Deborah Littlejohn, and Matt Peterson for all the Zoom happy hours and emergency text chains. Special thanks to Tsai Lu Liu for his leadership. I would also like to recognize all the wonderful students in our master's program in graphic design who provided a strong sounding board for this text, particularly my research assistants, Isabel Bo-Linn and Eryn Pierce.

Essential to this project were, of course, the many designers, researchers, and data scientists who graciously contributed to the book through interviews, essays, and projects. Your work inspires and delights, sketching out wonderful possibilities and essential guardrails for ML. Thanks, as well, to my industry collaborators over the years from SAS Analytics, IBM Watson Health, Advance Auto Parts, and many others. And special thanks to Keetra Dean Dixon for her amazing illustrations for this project. At Princeton Architectural Press, a special shout out to Jennifer Thompson and Kristen Hewitt for their thoughtful comments and ongoing support of the project. Working on this book has been a joy. So many possibilities lie before us in the coming years. Let's, together, grasp the ones that will lead our society forward.

Preface

"Be kind to each other. Because every action you make is what creates the future."—Mother Cyborg

Why should a designer care about machine learning (ML)? Fair question, right? After all, what do algorithms and predictions have to do with you? The answer grows more self-evident by the day.

Artificial intelligence (AI) is everywhere and has *already* transformed our profession. To be honest, it's going to steamroll right over us unless we jump aboard and start pulling the levers and steering the train in a human, ethical, and intentional direction. Here's another reason you should care: you can do amazing work by tapping the alien powers of nonhuman cognition. Think of ML as your future design superpower. Oh, and one last thing: industry and academia alike prize designers with a full understanding of this technology.

So, we have some studying to do. Together, we are going to take a journey. A journey across the three realms of ML. Each section considers ML and design through the lens of a central essay, a series of interviews, and several miniessays from a range of contributors. Want to break off from the path to dig deeper into how predictive algorithms work? An additional, more technically focused chapter follows these main sections. The book concludes with a short essay addressing the impact of ML upon design practice itself. In other words, in addition to the impact upon *what* we make, how might ML affect *how* we make?

Hopefully, this book will inspire you to take hold of ML, carefully but confidently. We should not trust a technology that has no true understanding of human consequences to take the lead. Instead, we human designers have to blaze the path forward ourselves. Let's get started.

Author's note: The development of artificial intelligence has a long, complex history. The main branch of AI in use today is machine learning—an approach to AI explained throughout this book. This text uses the terms *AI* and *ML* interchangeably with this in mind.

CHAPTER ONE

Peek Inside
the Black Box

Each day we generate data—terabytes of it. How have you produced data in the last month? In the last week? In the last hour? Did you write an email? Post a photo? Text a friend? Watch a streaming video? Wear an activity tracker? Drive through a traffic camera? As we move through our lives, we leave behind a garble of unstructured data—i.e., data not organized into ordered sets like spreadsheets or tables. Scholars claim that as much as 95 percent of all data is unstructured.[1] Machine learning (ML) enables a computer to derive meaning from all this unstructured data. Even now as you read, computers sift and categorize your data trails—both unstructured and structured—plunging deeper into who you are and what makes you tick.

$$q_{ij} = f\left(\text{shipping\_cost}_{ij},\ \text{shipping\_time}_{ij},\ \text{inventory\_match}_{ij},\ \ldots\right)$$

costs q	warehouses j		
	CA	TX	WI
clients i	0.235	0.172	0.624	...
	0.347	0.825	0.722	...
	0.533	0.874	0.193	...
	...		

$$\min_{a} \sum_i \sum_j a_{ij} q_{ij}$$

$$s.t.\quad a_{ij} \in \{0,1\},\ \forall i,j$$

$$\sum_j a_{ij} = 1\ \forall i$$

$$\sum_i a_{ij} < k_j\ \forall j$$

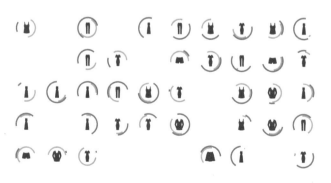

match feedback						explicit client features C_i			latent client features		
	?	0.83	?	0.54	?	0.47	0.23	...	?	?	...
	0.27	?	0.92	?	0.13	0.59	0.14	...	?	?	...
	?	?	0.85	0.76	?	0.62	0.90	...	?	?	...
S_j explicit style features	0.21	0.74	0.53	0.26	0.85						
	⋮	⋮	⋮	⋮	⋮						
latent style features	?	?	?	?	?						
	⋮	⋮	⋮	⋮	⋮						

FIG 1. STITCH FIX ALGORITHMS TOUR.
Through interactive storytelling, Stitch Fix visualizes its use of rich data to match clients with items of clothes, shoes, and accessories. The company combines algorithmic decision making with human skills—intuition, understanding context, and building relationships—to make shopping personal.

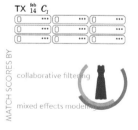

TX $^{\text{feb}}_{14}$ C_i

MATCH SCORES BY

collaborative filtering

mixed effects model

MACHINE LEARNING (ML): process of using algorithms to identify patterns from data and then make predictions or determinations about the world without explicit programming

UNSTRUCTURED DATA: data in its native format that does not have a predefined data model or is not organized in a pre-determined manner

STRUCTURED DATA: organized data that follows a standard-ized format

Today, computers intuit the world more like humans. When I enter a room, I don't learn about the room via a spreadsheet. Instead, I use my senses. I analyze images, sound, space, and movement. I take this information and make decisions based on what I find. Combining sensors (accelerometers, barometers, gyroscopes, proximity sensors, heart rate monitors, iris scanners, ambient light sensors, chemical and microbial sensors, electric noses) and other input devices (cameras, microphones, touch screens) with ML turns each trail of unstructured data into a richness of organized, coveted data resources. Imagine the impact of transforming vast quantities of previously unusable data— your data—into information that can be detected, digitally stored, and analyzed. Your politics, your personality, your sexuality, your next move. This is the future that is materializing right now.[2]

Without the sheer quantity of this data—data that used to be lost in the digital abyss—ML could not function effectively. Why is this? ML algorithms train using examples— bundles of data. The size and range of the examples deter-mine the subsequent accuracy rate.[3] This training process also requires masses of "compute," i.e., resources and processing power to fuel complex computation. According to journalist John Seabrook, "Innovations in chip design, network architec-ture, and cloud-based resources are making the total available compute ten times larger each year—as of 2018, it was three hundred thousand times larger than it was in 2012."[4] ML has taken off recently because both data collection and compute, along with accessible and affordable input devices and sensors, now flourish in our society.

THE ONSLAUGHT OF ALGORITHMS

But how does this mysterious ML stuff really work? Yesterday I checked my email, searched for an old high school friend online, used Waze to get across town—and tip me off to where the cops were—checked my Instagram feed, asked my Amazon Echo about the weather, and got a fraud detection alert from my credit card. Which of these activities involved ML? All of them. A prediction facilitated each of these interactions.

Put simply, ML consists of algorithms—in essence a set of task-oriented mathematical instructions—that use statistical models to analyze patterns in existing data and then make predictions based upon the results. They use data to compute likely outcomes. We can think of these algorithms as "Prediction Machines."[5] These algorithms might predict, for example, the buckwheat pillow that you are likely to buy or the Netflix series that you will binge next. They might predict the arrival time of an Uber or whether or not an email is spam (and whether you'll open it). They might predict the identity of a face or even the profile that will intrigue you on Tinder.

The magic of these predictions lies in the *learning*. ML algorithms not only analyze <u>historical data</u>, they also, once trained, make predictions about new data. For example, an email platform might employ ML to detect spam. The trained algorithms will be able to sleuth whether or not an email should go straight to the junk folder, not only in the original set of <u>training data</u> but also in new data—new emails—that enter the system.

Again, ML algorithms need to feed on a large quantity of training data to attain a high accuracy rate of predictions. Let's go back to humans for a moment as we consider this. In order to intuit things about the world, humans observe and interact with their environments. We noted earlier that this often occurs via unstructured data—movement, sound, images, etc. The wider the range of data that we encounter, the more complex our understanding grows. For example, imagine spending

HISTORICAL DATA: data collected automatically or manually about past events and circumstances

TRAINING DATA: initial data input to train models for use in ML

DATASET: a collection of data

MACHINE LEARNING ALGORITHMS

Analyze structured & unstructured data 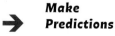 **Learn from the patterns detected** **Make Predictions**

your life in one small room, say your bedroom, interacting with only one person, perhaps your dad, over the course of your life. Everything you learned about human behavior would come from that single environment and that single person. Your understanding of the world would, subsequently, be very limited. The same is true for predictive algorithms. If, for instance, you build an ML system to identify a range of objects but only supply images of cars as training data, the system will subsequently classify every object it comes across as a car—because cars are all it knows. If training data only includes a narrow slice of examples, the system will only be able to make predictions that relate to a small range of possibilities.[6]

Input commands **Traditional programming**

Input data **ML algorithms**

How does ML compare to traditional programming? Traditional programming requires developers to enter explicit logic-based instructions—code—to produce behavior within a software system. In contrast, ML empowers the computer to observe and analyze behavior happening in the physical or digital world and then produce code to explain it.[7] We can say, "Hey, computer, make a prediction based upon these examples and then produce code that can apply that same prediction to future data."[8] This approach allows ML to take on predictions that are too complicated to address through line after line of logic-based instructions, like identifying a human face or determining the meaning of your last query to Alexa.

ADD A LITTLE PREDICTION AND SEE WHAT HAPPENS

When combined with intriguing datasets and powerful visions, ML algorithms can be quite transformative. Artists/activists Mimi Ọnụọha and Diana J. Nucera (a.k.a. Mother Cyborg) in their zine, *A People's Guide to AI*, compare this kind

> **"Abundant, cheap predictions are going to change the material that you're designing with, and you better get used to understanding how to work with it."**
> —Tony Chu, Facebook

of technology to salt—less interesting on its own but once added to food, "It can transform the meal."[9] Imagine that while watching a baseball game a prediction pops up that your favorite player is about to strike out and strand two batters on second and third bases. How would this kind of predictive power change the way you view the game or how players strategize their next move? Salt works as a metaphor for predictive algorithms on another level as well. Salt flavors many meals because it is cheap and widely available. As the cost of prediction technology drops, we will use it more and, as we increase use, its impact will compound.

Ajay Agrawal, Joshua Gan, and Avi Goldfarb point to this commodification of prediction in their book *Prediction Machines*. They look to artificial lights as a precedent. In the early 1800s, artificial light cost four hundred times more than it does today.[10] When the cost of artificial light plummeted, human work and family habits, as well as architecture and urban planning, changed dramatically. We could suddenly build rooms without windows and create large structures within which we could live and work both day and night. Hello, night shift.[11] We saw a similar phenomenon in the 1990s, when the internet lowered the "cost of distribution, communication, and search."[12] Whole industries, such as those for pagers, encyclopedias, and answering machines, disappeared or were revamped—video stores to Prime Video, travel agents to Google Travel—to take advantage of these new cheap capabilities. Consider the ramifications of the internet on music, catalog shopping, money transfer, postal services, archiving, etc. As the cost of utilizing ML algorithms drops, we can begin to imagine the impact of powering up prediction on many aspects of our lives.

DESIGNERS NEED TO JUMP INTO MACHINE LEARNING

ML needs designers. Our human-centered methods articulate human needs and desires in relation to the larger society. Too often data availability propels contemporary applications of ML rather than human need. In contrast to designers, who are trained to seek a desired future or "the 'right thing' to design," data scientists are trained to seek what can be accurately determined from the data at hand.[13] To look at this in a different way, let's envision that a data scientist and a designer are each throwing a dinner party. The data scientist determines the optimal meal by first evaluating available ingredients. What's fresh and in season? What's affordable? What's convenient? The designer starts by reviewing the guests' preferences. Any allergies? Any vegetarians? How hungry will they be? What do they crave? In contrast to the data scientist, the designer works back to the necessary ingredients and methods only after selecting an appropriate meal. If we don't acknowledge these disparate disciplinary goals and work collaboratively to engage ML, user-centered design—and human values—will fall to the wayside. We will frequently end up with optimized "meals" that no one wants to eat.

The responsibility of the designer to protect user interest and value has never been so imperative. As Aaron Weyenberg, director of research and development at TED, points out, ML shifts control away from the user. Multiple narratives blame the user for device addiction and failure to take proactive action in their own interest. But we don't often hear about the designer's "invisible hand meddling with the controls."[14] Designers have to own up to their role in the emerging predictive world. But it isn't easy. Designers work within an industry that utilizes behavioral research to direct user choices, face success incentives that downplay user well-being, and must operate within "the compounding effect of rapid optimization and deployment."[15] The tech industry browbeats designers to jump to the next "new" thing with little time for reflection. How can designers stand up for people in the face of such forces if most don't even understand the affordances of the technology?

HUMAN-CENTERED DESIGN: a problem-solving approach that looks to the human perspective in all steps of the process

DATA SCIENTISTS: analytical data experts who find trends and patterns and manage data

USER-CENTERED DESIGN: an iterative design approach in which designers concentrate on users and their needs throughout the design process

AFFORDANCES: the quality or property of an artifact that suggests to the user how it should be used

WHAT HAPPENS WHEN DESIGNERS POWER UP PREDICTION?

Now it's time for designers to enter the stage. Are you ready to take on ML? Yes, you are. Creating with ML pushes design—and designers—into an experiential space, whether you are creating a digital ad, an app, a digital publication, or a built environment. If you weren't focused on user experience before, you should be now. Every encounter with design becomes an interaction—and a user experience—that evolves over time as predictive algorithms learn from user behavior and the interface responds. For example, consider the AI-powered writing platform Grammarly. Grammarly constantly analyzes an individual's behavior, learning more about the user with each interaction. Eventually, the system knows an individual so well that it can complete the user's sentences for them, even advising on appropriate tone or sentiment based on its knowledge of the user's individual style.[16] Working with intelligent technology requires designers to plan for this kind of shifting experiential landscape in their projects. In this book I'm going to reference *user experience* and *interface*. Translate interface into the product appropriate to your own design practice. For example, you might design software, social media posts, cars, buildings, or installations. ML can bring each of these to life, opening your creative practice to new capabilities for personalizing experiences.

BUILT ENVIRONMENT: the human-made environment that provides setting for human activity

LET'S GET PERSONAL

What does it mean to *personalize* an experience? In relation to ML, this term suggests that the interface—whether digital display, website, app, virtual agent, or print-on-demand publication—uses predictive technology to determine what information or actions are most relevant to a user in that moment. Design researcher Liz Sanders popularized "useful, usable, and desirable" as the standard for creating a successful interaction in 2002.[17] Now we can ask, "Is this interface useful, usable, and desirable *to a certain individual in a particular context at a specific moment in time?*" Let's consider some ways to harness ML to do so.

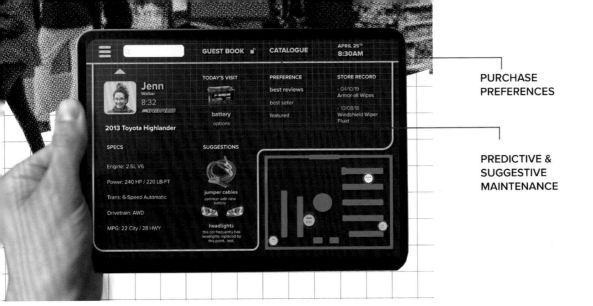

PURCHASE
PREFERENCES

PREDICTIVE &
SUGGESTIVE
MAINTENANCE

FIG 2. PREDICTIVE MAINTENANCE APPLICATION. In collaboration with an auto parts company, graphic design graduate students at North Carolina State University prototyped an intelligent system to anticipate each customer's automotive maintenance needs. The resulting application automatically generates recommendations after a vehicle identification system identifies the customer's vehicle in the store parking lot. Sales team members then share the recommendations with customers, blending AI intelligence with human interpersonal skills. Designed by North Carolina State University students: Harrison Lyman, Hannah Faub, Randa Hadi, and Matt Norton.

FIG 3. SEEING AI. This AI-powered app, created by Microsoft, narrates what it "sees" in the physical world to assist individuals with visual impairments. The tool can read short bits of type, including printed signs and posters, read currency, find and read barcodes to identify products, and even describe actions happening in the surrounding world.

First, ML algorithms can make recommendations. This is, perhaps, the most familiar and widely experienced ML capability. Amazon recommends products; TikTok recommends videos; Facebook recommends friends; Stitch Fix recommends outfits. [Fig. 1] Systems can make these recommendations based on product differences or similarities (you liked this white sequined jacket, so you might like another) or patterns of behavior (an urban millennial who works in accounting, listens to Solange weekly, watches twenty hours of TV a week, and invests in risky stocks will likely buy an Audi). Recommendation systems can also correct or emphasize mistakes, such as spelling/input errors or duplicate purchases, or even suggest future actions. In sum, recommendation systems can analyze behavioral and contextual data to suggest products, services, or behaviors that fit within the patterns that emerge.

CONTEXTUAL DATA: information and data that provides context for an event, person, or item

BIG DATA: large, complex datasets that are present in great volume, variety, and velocity, especially from new sources

We can see recommendations playing out across industries: retail, law enforcement, entertainment, military, finance, sports, and healthcare, among others. We can use predictive technology to care for our products, our homes, even our bodies. North Carolina State University design students recently partnered with an auto parts store to prototype a predictive automotive maintenance app. Based on the make and model of a customer's car, captured as individuals arrive at the store, the app parses big data to predict upcoming repairs, suggesting preemptive maintenance, preferable repair products, and even budgeting suggestions. [Fig. 2] Such an app could factor in hundreds of variables.

Algorithmic systems can recommend individualized paths of actions, but designers must construct the experience of communicating this knowledge to the user. IBM developer Tanmay Bakshi uses ML to prevent teen suicide. Instead of hoping a teen will call a helpline and talk to a human—unlikely behavior for a depressed Gen Z kid—he's developing an ML system to analyze teens' browser histories and lifestyle choices and then predict and proactively help those likely to commit suicide.[18] A professor of artificial intelligence and human-computer interaction at Carnegie Mellon University,

"AI requires people from all kinds of disciplines. Designers have a place in the room. We need to explore and play with these ideas. We need to be there because we will ask different questions."—Molly Wright Steenson, Carnegie Mellon University

John Zimmerman is building, along with his team, a decision support system that helps clinicians determine whether to implant an artificial heart in an individual. The support system includes a prediction for survival that is intended to be noticed only when it is in disagreement with what the clinicians plan to do.[19] [Fig. 4] Whether dealing with a depressed teen or a skeptical doctor, identifying a behavior pattern only provides true insight if the recipient understands and trusts the information an ML system places before them. How might designers create interfaces to support this transfer of knowledge? We will consider this issue of trust more in chapter three.

Personalizing an experience might also mean filtering information. Search engines, like Google, filter results so that each user can find what he/she seeks as quickly as possible. To cut down on noise—useless info—ML removes spam and duplicate content. At the same time, ML algorithms continually learn from each user's preferences and search history to improve the relevancy of results. This kind of filtering feeds Google's ad-targeting process or adjusts branded content.[20] When I search for "Viking ship-building techniques," my search results will differ from yours and so will the ads that target me. This is personalization.

Designers should consider, as a user approaches an interface, what information should be cast aside and what should be illuminated. Doctoral student Rachael Paine and a team of researchers are collaborating on a web-based hub for the caretakers of kids with rare diseases.[21] [Fig. 5] The hub's interface responds to the disease stage of each child by collecting data into buckets of focused information. By concentrating on what caretakers need to know at a particular moment in time, the interface prevents them from being overwhelmed with less

"If you want to make a device do something intelligent, you've got two options: You can program it, or it can learn. And people certainly weren't programmed, so we had to learn. This had to be the right way to go."
—Geoffrey Hinton, Google

immediate, highly distressing information like end-of-life care. We can consider this old-fashioned hierarchy on steroids. On the opposite end of the social impact spectrum, McDonald's plans to beguile customers with digital drive-in menus that detect an individual and then prioritize content and suggest complementary items in response to that individual's buying habits, time of day, local events, weather patterns, etc.[22] When a consumer looks at the menu, it will look back and then adapt. You love the Sausage, Egg & Cheese McGriddle, so here are three special combo deals, just for you. And, by the way, it's hot, so we will throw in an iced latte. In other words, fast food will get even faster.

In 2011, author and activist Eli Pariser gave a TED talk entitled "Beware Online 'Filter Bubbles.'" Pariser brought to the public's attention the dangers of creating information flows that "leave us all isolated in a web of one." He warned that we've moved "from human gatekeepers to algorithmic ones" and that "the algorithms don't yet have the kind of embedded ethics that [human] editors did."[23] If computers are getting more human, they are humans without a conscience or morality. Pariser pleads with big tech, like Google and Facebook, to encode responsibility into these algorithms and hand over more content control to the user. Media theorists, such as Douglas Rushkoff, Geert Lovink, Shoshana Zuboff, and Yuval Noah Harari, have also tackled this topic as evidence swells that our society is growing ever more divisive.[24] Filter Bubbles have become Experience Bubbles as algorithmic prediction has expanded beyond search engines. Most designers can't recode ML algorithms, but we can carefully consider how capabilities like recommendations and filtering can positively empower users rather than double down on negative impulses.[25]

FILTER BUBBLES: state of intellectual isolation that can result from personalized searches and algorithms

GATEKEEPING: process of controlling and limiting access to information

FIG 4. CARDIAC HEALTH RISK STRATIFICATION SYSTEM. John Zimmerman and his team at Carnegie Mellon University created this interface to help cardiologists decide if they should implant a mechanical heart. The AI uses historic patient records to predict how long this patient would likely survive post implant, displayed as a survival curve in the upper-right-hand corner of the interface. Interface design by Qian Yang, PhD.

FIG 5. RARE DISEASE INFO HUB. Design researcher Rachael Paine collaborated with North Carolina State University colleagues in computer science to create an intelligent information hub for caretakers of kids with rare diseases. Paine prototyped an intelligent navigation system that filtered data collected by the ML algorithms into "buckets" of information. These buckets shared the info with caretakers at the appropriate stage of their child's illness.

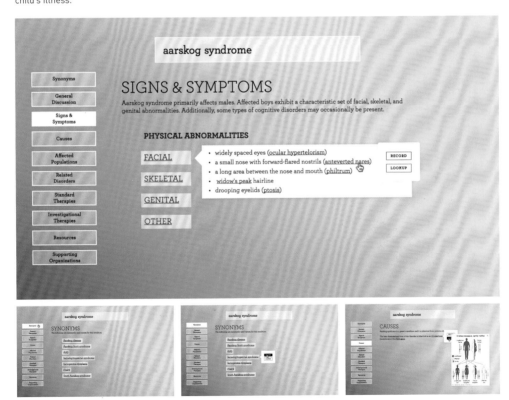

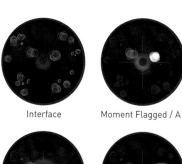

Interface · Moment Flagged / A

Moment Flagged / B · Side Blur

Portrait Blur · Bubble Blur

Persona: Andrea, an HR assistant, is profoundly deaf with two cochlear implants.

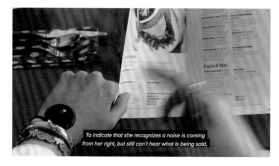

To indicate that she recognizes a noise is coming from her right, but still can't hear what is being said,

and triggers Bubble Blur, effectively shielding her table from background noise with a cardioid microphone.

FIG 6. HEARU. This wearable device prototype interfaces with cochlear implants and hearing aids via Bluetooth to adjust microphones to optimal settings thus facilitating small-group conversation. The ML-powered interface continually optimizes the experience based upon user feedback. Designed by North Carolina State University Master in Graphic Design students: Shadrick Addy, Jessye Holmgren-Sidell, Matt Lemmond, and Krithika Sathyamurthy.

[restaurant noises and loud conversation commence]
Narrator - Everyone, including Andrea,

This helps train the machine learning algorithm to switch to Side Blur in instances similar to this.

THE ANTICIPATION OF DESIGN

Each of these examples suggest that we are entering a world of *anticipatory design*.[26] Anticipatory design is a UX (user experience) pattern that predicts user behavior and responds preemptively. In essence, anticipatory design lessens or removes user choice to increase convenience and relevance. For example, the ML system driving a conferencing platform might notice that each time a child approaches your laptop during a virtual office meeting, you turn off your camera. So, instead of waiting for you, the software might begin automatically adjusting the camera whenever your kid runs toward the screen. Or imagine that each time you shop for clothes, the software only shows options available in your size and in the colors you prefer, without you needing to apply filters. We can envision a day in the near future in which products will ship to us *before* we even know we want them—anticipatory shipping. Amazon is exploring this concept right now.[27] We also see anticipatory design playing out in healthcare. Imagine the design of an AI platform that detects and diagnoses a disease *before* you complain of symptoms and automatically supplies preemptive treatment.[28] This kind of user experience no longer requires direct input from the user but rather gathers data and analyzes the resulting patterns.

Anticipatory Design **No direct user input**

Following a pattern of anticipatory design, an interface could seamlessly adjust to user needs and reduce <u>cognitive load</u>. Imagine an interface that detects, for example, a specific kind of <u>visual impairment</u> and automatically adjusts the screen layout and color-contrast ratio to increase visibility in response to a particular user's condition. Recently, DeepMind tested viable prototypes for an ML tool that scans and analyzes images of the retina and then, in about 30 seconds, shares a detailed diagnosis and urgency score.[29] It's not hard to envision how such a diagnostic tool could feed a responsive interface.

COGNITIVE LOAD: the amount of working memory used to perform various tasks

VISUAL IMPAIRMENT: a decreased ability to see to a degree that causes problems not fixable by usual means such as glasses

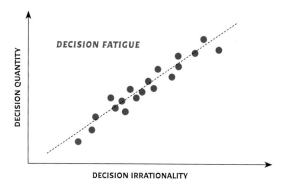

DECISION FATIGUE

DECISION QUANTITY

DECISION IRRATIONALITY

ML provides rich possibilities for detecting and adapting to unique needs. Intuitive seamless experiences can seem, in the words of theorist David Rose, "enchanted," the stuff of fairy tales. Rose decries what he describes as a "terminal world" in which "the machine sits on idle, waiting for your orders."[30] Instead, ML could instill into our devices and environments just enough agency that we don't have to make frequent requests.

In addition to the sheer magic of an interface that knows intuitively what we need, such an intelligent interface could take away some of the endless distracting choices of modern life. Each day, we make around thirty-five thousand decisions. The danger here lies not just in stress but also in decision fatigue.[31] As product designer Joël van Bodegraven notes, "The more decisions we make, the less rational they become."[32] This might not matter when we are deciding which toaster to buy, but it could have a huge impact when buying a house or diagnosing a patient or taking a crucial test. On one hand, making decisions on behalf of users takes away their ability to choose for themselves. This lack of choice intensifies the Experience Bubble discussed earlier. On the other hand, when algorithms make some choices, the user, ideally, can focus on making better decisions for the essential choices that remain. To make this even harder for the designer, the cost of getting this trade-off wrong is high. We've all been frustrated by machines making decisions that conflict with our actual goals. Mobile phones incorrectly autocorrecting words irritate—and sometimes mortally embarrass—users everywhere. Researcher Graham Dove et al. characterizes this as the "automation debate between 'do it for me' and 'do it myself.'"[33] As predictive algorithms infiltrate the majority of designed experiences, the stakes of getting this right will only go up.

CLUMSY, LIKE A TODDLER

In addition to the delicate balance between giving and eliminating user choice, anticipatory design presents another challenge to designers: predictive algorithms require multiple user interactions to learn users' preferences and behaviors well enough to accurately predict their needs. This is called "the cold start problem." The interface must communicate that the system is learning and improving over time, or the user will grow frustrated and leave early in the process. To engage the user, the system must demonstrate individualized behavior immediately, but—paradoxically—the system needs extended interactions to do so effectively. To combat this, the designer has to set realistic expectations around interface behavior up front. Past experiences with interfaces have trained users to expect reliable, useful behavior upon entry. Instead, individuals need to begin to view an intelligent interface as if it's a toddler—clumsy at first but quickly gaining agility and knowledge over time.[34]

Despite the difficulties around engaging the user before the system knows them well, the gradual optimization of ML experiences can become one of an intelligent interface's greatest strengths. As researcher Qian Yang asserts, "Data-driven personalization can build and maintain long-term customer relationships with a view toward creating lifetime value."[35] If the user can just hang in there, the interaction will get better and better, resulting in thick, resilient connections between user and platform/brand. The more time users invest, the more the interface will, ideally, attune to their needs: a clear reward for investing time.

Patterns of anticipatory design are still in infancy. Some designers are exploring playful models that might complement or even replace more typical frictionless interactions. Interaction professor Philip van Allen and design theorist Betti Marenko critique current models of anticipatory design as predictable and mechanical. These interactions, they argue, narrow down user choices too stridently, forcing the user into a dull, unimaginative user experience.[36] They suggest, instead, that we might use *animistic design* as "an alternative to the hyper-designed-experience approach that we're all suffering from right now in the experience economy and the attention economy."[37]

Animistic design embraces uncertainty and unpredictability by introducing intelligent objects with their own sense of agency and idiosyncratic personalities. These autonomous devices or actants can disrupt and subvert user expectations rather than simply anticipate, manage, and fulfill. In two such prototyped explorations, AniThings and Little Data Wranglers, a single user interacts with intelligent objects. The resulting emergent milieu becomes "a kind of extended mind." AniThings and Little Data Wranglers act as collaborators with the user, introducing unexpected points of view, perhaps even acting as "agent[s] of creativity-inducing disruption."[38] [Fig. 11] Van Allen and Marenko's work suggests that existing anticipatory design models represent only a sliver of what's possible. To push ML technology toward novel applications that truly benefit humans, rather than just making it easier to buy that new blow-up hot tub, designers need to get their minds and hands around ML. They need to be able to noodle around with it.

MACHINE LEARNING AS A DESIGN MATERIAL

Designers struggle to "sketch" with a technology as invisible and intangible as ML. And, according to van Allen, "if we can't sketch with AI as designers, it's like our right arm is cut off. We have to be able to play around."[39] Carnegie Mellon human-computer interaction professor John Zimmerman explains, "When I teach a designer, I can give them cardboard

FRICTIONLESS INTERACTIONS: a seamless experience where the user has no need to put in extra effort to complete a task

AUTONOMOUS: existing or capable of existing independently without outside control

ACTANT: a person or object that plays an active role in a narrative

DESIGN MATERIAL: as in the work of Donald Schön, a reflective conversation with a problem through the use of specific materials

FIG 7. DELFT AI TOOLKIT. Interaction design professor Philip van Allen created this no-code programming environment to give designers easy access to ML. Designers can initially use the tool to simulate an AI system in 3D with Unity. They can observe the system's behavior in this virtual space so that they might tweak it before making a physical robot.

FIG 8. WOEBOT. Woebot Health, founded by Alison Darcy, a Stanford University–trained clinical research psychologist, enables individuals to access mental healthcare via this chatbot. Using CBT, or cognitive behavioral therapy, as a therapeutic framework, the bot helps people cope with life's challenges by using brief conversations to ask people how they're feeling and what is going on in their lives, then delivers useful tools for the mood and the moment.

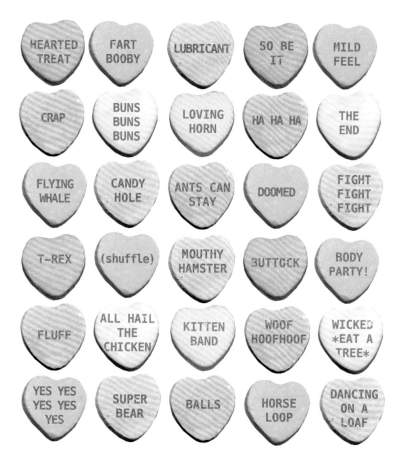

FIG 9. CANDY HEARTS. Janelle Shane's experiments playfully tease out all the ways algorithms can "get things wrong." She jumps unafraid into the algorithmic training process, in this instance training a neural network to generate candy heart messages. Shane has also trained algorithms to invent recipes, paint colors, pickup lines, and cat names.[40]

> *"I've long felt that technology is a material of design. Understanding the grain of the material of whatever you work with is key to being a good designer."*
> —Philip van Allen, ArtCenter College of Design

and say, 'Make a stool; make a hat.' They'll then learn what cardboard can do. But I can't send somebody to play with machine learning like that."[41] We can see this barrier in the limited number of designers currently engaging with the technology.[42] Since we can't cut it and fold it like cardboard, how do we engage with ML as a design material?[43] One method is to focus not on how the tech works but rather on its capabilities.

Zimmerman finds that the majority of design students don't know what is possible. "Or if they think to use ML, they use it in a way that is so magical that they're envisioning things that can't be built."[44] His team often uses a system called matchmaking that's the inverse of the typical user-centered process. Zimmerman explains:

> With user-centered design, we start by finding a person. We study them. Then we say, here's what technology could do for you—but that assumes the designers *know* what the technology can do. In order to build that understanding of what's possible, our team works the other way. We say, for example, here's a two-class text classifier. What are all the things you might do with that and who might you do it for? Sometimes we give them a list of 400 occupations to get designers to think broadly across a whole bunch of different people…by doing that, that's sort of like cutting cardboard….We are trying to get the students to see the world more algorithmically as a way to say, "Don't just try to imagine the things that would be really hard for machine learning to do, but focus on where you could use it every day on the things that you're currently making, where is there an opportunity?"[45]

This method helps acclimate design students to the capabilities of ML rather than the technical details. Zimmerman asserts: "Like anything, the more you sketch with it, the more comfortable you are thinking of it. Suddenly you have a bunch

TEXT CLASSIFICATION: one of the fundamental tasks in natural language processing, the assigning of tags or categories to text according to its content

"ML is the new UX. I envision UX practitioners leveraging machine learning as a design material creatively and thoughtfully, guiding users and technologists toward a deliberative ML-mediated future."—Qian Yang, Cornell University

of exemplars in your mind and abstractions for the capabilities." Zimmerman wants his design students to first come up with ideas that are buildable. "Because," he explains, "if you can't do that, none of the other stuff matters....Design teams right now never propose ideas for machine learning. They get ideas from a data science team, mostly for things no one would want." Zimmerman wants his design students to "innovate on ML's face of possibility."[46]

So, one approach to digging into ML is for designers to identify existing capabilities and then apply them in novel ways. How else might designers work with ML as a design material? Van Allen created the Delft AI Toolkit, a drag-and-drop, visual programming environment that enables designers to quickly build the interaction and behavior of a proposed AI system.[47] Initially, designers can use the tool kit to simulate an interaction in 3D. This simulation process means they don't have to commit immediately to the training and implementing of an actual ML algorithm. Instead, they can use a "personality control panel to shape the system's behavior and data sources" and "a visual marionette system so the designer can 'Wizard-of-Oz' AI behaviors in real time while observing users."[48] [Fig. 7] Van Allen's software helps designers to jump in and gain hands-on experience with algorithmic behavior and user responses before investing time and expertise into model training.

Zimmerman's methods and van Allen's tool kit both help designers prototype intelligent interfaces that utilize ML capabilities. The ML algorithms themselves function in a traditional data science way: the statistical model tries to make "accurate" predictions by representing "some truth about the world." In other words, algorithms work in the way that they were designed to work: the system makes a prediction

EXEMPLARS: a typical example or excellent model

WIZARD-OF-OZ METHOD: an iterative methodology where an experimenter simulates the behavior of a prototype to garner user feedback

MODEL TRAINING: supplying training data and tweaking a machine learning model so that it might learn to make predictions on new data

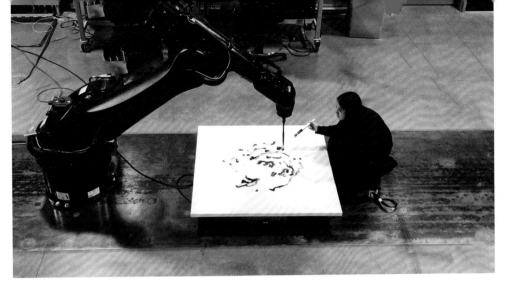

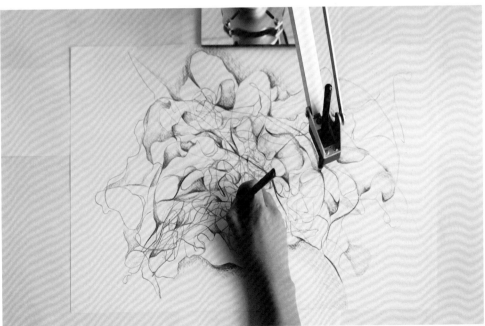

FIG 10. D.O.U.G._2. (DRAWING OPERATIONS UNIT: GENERATION 2). Artist and researcher Sougwen Chung explores how a human artist might collaborate with an ML system to symbiotically produce work. In this rendition, Chung trains an algorithmic system to learn from the visual style of an artist's previous drawings and then translate that style into gesture and color palette. A robotic arm then pulls from this knowledge to draw in concert with the artist. Chung questions artistic identity and self-perception through such human-machine duets.

> *"Once you train a model, you have access to explore the space and see...behaviors that you didn't imagine when you were setting up the machine learning system."*
> —Rebecca Fiebrink, University of the Arts London

of likely future behavior based on the data at hand. The designers then find innovative applications for the technology, thus expanding the potentialities of intelligent interface design.

But there are other ways to think about designers engaging with ML as a design material. Designers can also engage with training data more directly. Rather than data as Ground Truth, "[data] can be a way for people to communicate ideas and intentions." In 2008, computer scientist Rebecca Fiebrink asked: "How can ML support people's existing creative practices? Expand people's creative capabilities?"[49] She developed Wekinator, an open-source software platform, with the original goal of making predictive algorithms useful to experimental musicians and composers. Recognizing that "potential sources of data are everywhere"—social media, smartphones with sensors, Arduinos, cameras, microphones, etc.—she developed a platform that empowers people to input and quickly train their own data. Through this software, the human and the data can converse, pushing and pulling one another in novel directions. Imagine, for example, rapidly training a model to recognize a spectrum of physical gestures and then correlate those gestures to musical notes. By gesturing, you could then compose music on the fly. Wekinator's real-time data training capabilities allow creatives to prototype and experiment using a tacit, embodied approach, allowing the unexpected to surface.

Ultimately, Fiebrink wants to "open up new creative relationships between humans and machines." She asserts that ML will not replace human creativity but rather people "will take advantage of algorithms."[50] New tools, such as Google's Teachable Machine, Artbreeder, and Runway ML, are encouraging nonexperts to do so. Advances in Generative Adversarial Networks (GANS) have opened up exciting

GROUND TRUTH: the reality that you want your model to predict as accurately as possible

OPEN-SOURCE: original source code that is freely available and may be redistributed and modified in line with user requirements

ARDUINO: an open-source digital platform or board, and the corresponding software, that allows users to program interactive electronic objects

TACIT: knowledge that is understood or implied without being verbalized or written down

GENERATIVE ADVERSARIAL NETWORKS (GANS): a machine learning system in which two neural networks— the Generator model and the Discriminator Model—compete to improve the quality of their results.

possibilities for creatives, particularly around image and style translation and generation. Artists and designers like Janelle Shane, Helena Sarin, Mario Klingemann, and Sougwen Chung are creating vibrant work through direct access to training data and models. [Figs. 9, 10] Designer Andreas Refsgaard, for example, makes "weird fun stuff" like Sound-Controlled Intergalactic Teddy, "an infinite runner game where you use your voice and sounds to control Teddy's movements," and Poems About Things, a project that generates poetry using Google's Suggest API in response to objects labeled by an image recognition system. He uses the "mistakes" made by algorithms as fodder for his work.[51] These creatives are, in a sense, playfully viewing the world through the eyes of an algorithm and then using the resulting alien perspective to inform their own creative practice.

IN SUM: *THE RACE IS ON*

Design is racing to match the speed at which industry is adopting ML technology. The cost of the technology drops even as the amount of data swells. "Prediction machines" surround us, recommending, filtering, and profiling human behaviors and desires. Anticipatory design portends friction-less interactions rapidly morphing to meet individual needs. With great potential comes great risk as designers struggle to balance intuitive smart responses with reduced human control. Designers need to jump into the ML fray now and cultivate critical design practices that advocate for humans. To do so, they need to understand the basic concepts and capabilities of the technology so that they might begin to "sketch" out the future using this strange and exhilarating new design material.

JOHN ZIMMERMAN, PHD
Interview

As Tang Family Professor of Artificial Intelligence and Human-Computer Interaction at Carnegie Mellon University (CMU), John Zimmerman investigates, among other areas, the blending of human and machine intelligence. He delves into how designers might work with machine learning as a design material, pushing the capabilities of the medium into unexplored spaces.

How have your students reacted to working with machine learning?

There's a lot of frustration because students want a method more like user-centered design, one you can cookbook. That doesn't exist yet. And they want tools and resources that don't exist. Part of the reason that we're teaching this is to construct those things. At CMU, we're also saying we want students who are willing to design things we know you can't design. We're giving you an impossible task. And from that, we're going to figure out what works. I think the design field always does that: it reinvents itself based on whatever challenge it's faced with. Generally, it's not students asked to do the reinventing, but that's what we're doing.

Why is it difficult for design students to experiment with machine learning?

With machine learning, you don't know what errors the system will produce until you make it. With a paper prototyping mindset, you think you're going to find all of the big problems to reduce the risk of making something people won't want. There's absolutely no way to do that with machine learning. With this material, you can't simulate what will go wrong. You can simulate it working perfectly, but that's actually not the part you care about. You care about how to change the interaction in support of those wrong directions— directions that are unpredictable. We did a system that would read incoming emails, select a form, and then fill out a form. You would send an email and say, "Oh, can you guys please update my phone number?" It would pull the contact and fill it in. One of the errors our ML system made was it assumed that someone wanted to change their phone number *and* their last name: Scott Smith sent this message to change his phone number. The system chose Scott Jones, changed his last name to Smith, and changed his phone number. None of the humans that were approving the agent's work noticed the last name had been changed. This introduced a huge error into this dataset, an error no human would ever have made. How do I get designers to recognize the nonhuman type of intelligence that would produce this kind of error?

What are some difficulties that you've found working with data scientists and designers?

For a long time, designers have viewed themselves as user advocates. Now data scientists come to the conversation as user advocates but with a different view of the user and what that means. In that conversation, when they are not united, the data scientist shows up with a bunch of evidence. The designers show up with a bunch of hunches—they have informed intuition, but it's impossible to prove intuition. What I loved about the designers we saw in industry was that they were good at working with data. If I was at a place like Google and I was interested in search, I would actually have search data that I had access to. The design teams would form an intuition, like, "I think we could do this." And then they could look at the data to see: "Can I, by myself, begin to see a pattern that would be learnable? Is there something in there?" They weren't doing data mining. They weren't looking for covariance. They were hunch driven, but they could do this querying on their own before going to talk to the data scientists.

There was appreciation on both sides that you're not wasting each other's time. What we're really trying to reach is a point where those two groups can work together to come up with something neither of them could think of on their own—interdisciplinary collaboration leading to solutions.

What do designers need to know about the impact of machine learning on their practice?

There's a terrible, limiting mindset that human-to-human interaction is the pinnacle we're striving for, but we all know people don't necessarily interact super well. Computation has superhuman abilities. How and when can we get at that in a way that's not disturbing? We've been doing some work that we call "robot re-embodiment." When can and should a robot consciousness jump from body to body? We saw things like, I go to the DMV and, when I check in, a robot checks me in. But then when I walk to the first station to get my photo, that robot—in a sense it's mine—jumps there and meets me there. But now it has a camera. Then it can jump to whatever the next thing is. In our research, people liked the singularity of that experience of being taken care of.

We did the same thing in the context of a hospital. People were unhappy because a robot that checks them in couldn't possibly be smart enough to take their MRI. That's a human view of the world: social status is intermixed with expertise. How does our design work surface these invisible boundaries? Brain hopping, not a problem. Nobody struggles with that. But crossing social status lines—that's wrong. We're interested in designers who are working in these spaces. How do we surface and share this knowledge to create design patterns that help us define what these things are?

JOANNA PEÑA-BICKLEY
Interview

Head of research and design of Alexa Devices at Amazon, Joanna Peña-Bickley is known as the mother of Cognitive Experience Design. As an activist, artist, and inventor, she inspires the C-Suite to develop meaningful, inclusive experiences within our increasingly AI-powered world.

How does your understanding of design intersect with your current position working with Alexa devices?

Designers have a mission to be the ethical voice of empathy for our customers on our product teams. We are partnered with product, not in service to our product teams. As you know, in most organizations, design is subservient to engineering or subservient to a product organization. At Amazon, we are full and equal partners, and we take a multidisciplinary approach to design. The thing that we all have in common is that we understand the fourteen hundred and forty minutes in a day are precious. So, when you choose to purchase a product that we have created, that product ultimately needs to accelerate your intelligence and improve the time that you have with the people that you care about. I don't need to answer twenty emails at the dinner table when I can have my device create a mood and behavioral experience through the perfect music and lighting. I can put my phone down and have a real conversation.

In our on-the-go experiences, voice should be the primary interaction, so that we're not tethered to our phones. One of my team's favorite inventions this year has been the Echo Buds, which bring the power of Alexa to your earbuds. We have spent too much time as designers tethering people to devices as opposed to facilitating their way through the world in an individualized and secure way. There is this tension in the assumption that voice is up and coming. Voice has been here for twenty some years. We just didn't include it.

Designers have been humble enough to get their hands dirty with technology and experiment in a manner that transforms our discipline from static content creators or visual creators or visual pattern creators to understanding that some of these patterns could get smarter over time—and then looking for new interfaces, whether that be voice or others. I think one of the more exciting ones right now is brain interface. I have worked with the disability community for some time, working with veterans, for example, to augment

"We owe people who hire us not just our labor but our counsel."
—Joanna Peña-Bickley

> *"The very discipline of design is shifting toward understanding and holding the golden thread of data and code for everything that we do."*
> —Joanna Peña-Bickley

their physical experience in the world. If leveraged correctly, brain interface stands to augment humans when a capability is challenging. We need designers, not just engineers, in this process because we're designing for humans.

I'm interested in what you're saying about brain interface and disability. I've seen your commitment to inclusion over the course of your career.

I couldn't get any more intersectional. I am a highly dyslexic Latinx Jewish woman from the state of Texas. Part of it is a self-survival story. There's a lot of shame around cognitive disabilities. We used to stigmatize people, excluding them and placing them in separate classes. Having dyslexia didn't mean I wasn't smart or capable. I just couldn't read. Once I got to a point that I was able to teach myself the ability, I became a voracious reader. Right now, we're in a bit of a buzzword bingo with accessibility. We see companies claim inclusive design when they're just checking an accessibility box. Inclusive design is about being inclusive from the ground up. I am so proud of Amazon in this way. Not perfect, but we try to be.

I talk to a lot of designers who want to design for people with disabilities, but not with. And that's over; you can't do it that way. Solutions and ideas come to the table because you have somebody who is deaf or has a physical disability or low vision or blindness. I have made it my mission to give underrepresented people voices now that I have a platform—to ensure that they are included on my team. Not just in our user groups, but on my team. My team must reflect the customer base that we serve.

Can you speak about the synergies between Alexa devices and inclusion?

They're coming together because we have a robust and remarkable disability community that's included on our design team. These things don't happen by accident. I work with leaders from both the deaf and hard-of-hearing and low-vision communities where multimodal experiences are important. Even in our voice-only experiences, the design of LED lights becomes super important. The accessibility intent was always there in the design. To hear people actually use the technology in this way becomes something refreshing and remarkable. There are hundreds of use cases in which our devices address disability. It happens quite naturally and with intention. One of the design principles inside my organization is "inclusive by design."

REBECCA FIEBRINK, PHD
Interview

Rebecca Fiebrink is a reader at the Creative Computing Institute of the University of the Arts London. Her machine-learning-based, open-source software, the Wekinator, empowers humans to generate real-time interactive systems by demonstrating human actions. Fiebrink works frequently with human-centered and participatory design processes to understand how users might more intuitively create through machine learning.

What do you think is important for designers to understand about machine learning?
The way I think about machine learning now as a design tool is different from the way I was taught to think about it as a computer science student. The conventional approach is to think about machine learning, especially supervised learning, as a set of tools for faithfully modeling data. But, in my work, I've changed to thinking about data as a way for people to communicate with computers. This is especially important when either you're trying to capture embodied practice or tacit knowledge or any number of things that are important to people but are difficult for people to describe to one another in their native language, let alone describe to a computer in programming code or a mathematical model. In building a musical instrument or teaching a computer to listen to music or voice, often the easiest thing we can do as creators is demonstrate, "OK, here's how I want to move around," "here's how something should sound," or "here's how something should look." If we were communicating that to another person, we would move or we would use examples. We wouldn't try to write them a mathematical equation because we don't think like that. We can look at machine learning as just an algorithmic tool that helps us communicate to computers using examples. And that can make design much easier to engage in as a person. It can make it faster to build something and less frustrating.

Your process of building something digitally is playful and fun because you're demonstrating things. You're changing its behavior by demonstrating rather than continually stepping back from the creative part and trying to debug code or revise some math. Once you think about data as an interface for communication, rather than something that's a "ground truth" that you have to model, then a lot of other things change as well. Like what should you put in an interface for using machine learning? How should you evaluate whether a machine learning algorithm is doing what you want? Who should have the power to train a machine learning model and why?

Wekinator allows for a certain element of the unexpected, right? What do those moments mean to creatives?

The element of the unexpected is one of the most important things to people who have used Wekinator in creative work. You could contrast that to the way that you might build similar systems without machine learning, which is usually by programming. If you build things by programming, when surprises happen you get a compilation error or it just doesn't do anything. That's a surprise that's not likely to be creatively useful. But if you're using machine learning, you have a working machine-learning pipeline, which means you're training on some data and building a model that you can run. Those models are going to output something in the domain that you're working in. So if you're controlling sounds, you're going to get some sounds. If you're controlling animation, you're going to get some animations. At the least, when something goes wrong, you're confronted with an error that has the possibility to surprise you.

Can you talk about your experiences using Wekinator to create individualized tools for people with disabilities?

I've done two projects recently with people with disabilities, grounded primarily in music. We had a desire in both to build interfaces that people could interact with in meaningful ways to make music, regardless of physical limitations.

In the Sound Lab project, we trained our interfaces in advance, but we trained them so they had a wide variety of possible sounds. You could get variation in sound by moving really big or by moving really small. We had controllers so that people could move in all sorts of ways and you would get a sound no matter what. In Sound Lab we didn't want to take a lot of time to retrain each person as they sat down and, instead, made instruments that responded no matter how they were played—we were able to allow people to come up with personalized gestures. They'd move around and find something that was both comfortable and sounded cool.

In the Sound Control project, our goal was to make it so that teachers and therapists could make musical instruments that were entirely bespoke to each child. The teachers and therapists went beyond that and were making a new instrument every five to ten minutes with the kids. It wasn't, "Oh, I'm going to build you an instrument and you're going to learn how to play it." But more like, "I'll build an instrument so that we can explore your range of motion in your arms today. And we can do some arm games. And then when we get tired of that, I'll build you another."

You could build interfaces that were both customized to anybody's motions, no matter what kind of motion they're able to do, and more recognizable to the child as something that they were controlling. One of the learning outcomes that was important to the teachers and therapists was just giving kids a chance to have some agency over their environment that they recognized as agency, given that that doesn't always happen for them during the school day.

ALEX FEFEGHA
Interview

Cofounder and head of making at the London-based innovation studio Comuzi, Alex Fefegha strives to build a better world through radical creativity. He has examined algorithmic racial and gender bias, prototyped alternative intelligent futures, and created experiences that invite the public to dig into artificial intelligence.

What inspired you to work with algorithmic bias originally?

As a student, I came across a ProPublica piece written by Julia Angwin. She explored the system used to identify re-offenders. In her research she found that Black offenders were seen by the system as more likely to re-offend than white offenders even though that wasn't actually the case. She touches on how when you got arrested, you were given a survey. This survey doesn't ask your race, but particular questions could be linked to other demographics. Some of the questions were, "Has your mom or dad ever been divorced? Have any of your friends gone to prison? Have you ever gone to prison?" You know, normally when I talk about this stuff, I talk about growing up in South London, Peckham. If someone were to ask me if some of my friends had gone to prison, I could say, yes, some of my friends have. That was just a thing growing up in the area.

So I looked at the design. The algorithm was doing what it was instructed to do. All an algorithm does is make predictions and probabilities. It examines the past to present a future perspective. I thought that it wasn't the algorithm, and, in that case, it was actually the survey itself. From a design perspective, how was the survey designed to get this information? I looked at the design of the data—where the data was coming from. And that is initially how I started to explore gender bias as well.

What's it like to work in the AI (artificial intelligence) design space?

I think the hardest thing about working in this space is expectation versus reality. As a designer working with AI, it's important to not get lost in expectation. You've got to make sure you have a reason for the technology—especially when companies want to leverage AI to achieve a goal. Companies don't always know what they are hiring you to do, but they hand you a brief saying they want this thing to be "AI-powered." Design can help companies articulate what is real and what is not real.

Mozilla recently commissioned a project with Comuzi that we are calling Invisible Masks. Mozilla wanted us to just explore a topic that we were interested in. And we were interested in facial recognition

"All the algorithm does is makes predictions and probabilities....
It examines the past to present a future perspective."—Alex Fefegha

because in London the metropolitan police have been exploring new tools, such as a gang matrix, a database of people identified as most likely to be in gangs. Being in the matrix doesn't even necessarily mean that you are in a gang. Maybe your bro is in a gang. Amnesty International did a campaign about how their basic dataset was actually racist. Invisible Masks was inspired by an academic paper in which people were trying to use infrared light to deter facial recognition cameras. The facial recognition in your phones and Apple ID screens are now using infrared light to scan your face. The concept of the masks is that a hood admits red light on a particular part of the human face so that you can hopefully evade facial recognition. Obviously, every facial recognition system that might be used commercially is trained from a different model. So you might be able to disrupt one, but you won't be able to disrupt all. However, we decided to create a prototype of this thing and get people to try it out in the public. And for us it was like, how do you have conversations about surveillance culture? In our mind, we were making this thing based on the idea of having a voice. There will be communities who reject living under surveillance. I hope that those communities will be well equipped in order to decide to protect themselves. So that was our conversation: particular communities will not approve of surveillance especially if this high-end new tech gets you wrong all the time. They will need to be creative in order to disrupt it.

I love the idea of using design to protect yourself. If we jump ahead, say, twenty years, and envision a positive future for machine learning in the UK, what would that look like?
It's a question of the driver. Capitalism tells us to always try to implement something new and engage our customers. We keep the customers. We make the money. And that drives innovation. Maybe sometimes we get to question the impact of all this stuff. Often the question I ask is, "Do we need half of it? Do we need to further enhance everything in a push to perform?" My positive future is when we will be able to say, "You know what, let's put this stuff on hold and try to solve some of the human problems that we have." A future in which communities have the agency to protect themselves. I come from a community where our relationship with policing has been very interesting. Why, for example, do we need to use machine learning in the justice system to identify re-offenders? Is it because there is financial difficulty and people are overworked? Are we using machine learning to analyze data faster than humans can? What are the limitations? Let's figure it out and set some boundaries.

Animistic Design
Philip van Allen

As a professor in the Media Design Practices MFA program at ArtCenter College of Design, Philip van Allen pursues new educational models, technologies, and tools for teaching and learning. His research focuses on the intersection of artificial intelligence (AI), tangible interaction, media, and networks, and the new ecologies these create.

I've been exploring the animistic design approach to interaction over the last eight years, and it uses the natural tendency of people to perceive inanimate things as being alive. In adults, this perception is understood to be a fiction, yet it remains a powerful metaphor that can open up the black box of "smart" entities.

HETEROGENEOUS MULTIPLICITY

By generating a multiplicity of heterogeneous, autonomous personalities that interact with each other, humans, and shared data, a rich ecology is created. This ecology changes over time as conversations occur, material is introduced, patterns are learned, and relationships are developed.

The goal for the designer, then, is to create a rich, serendipitous, and diverse milieu in which the independent things and people are conversing, exchanging, competing, provoking, making, and collaborating well.

COLLEAGUES NOT CONSCRIPTS

This approach contrasts with the solutionist captain-and-conscripts relationship that people seem to have with their devices—we want our things to accomplish our tasks, so we issue commands. This is, of course, valuable at times. But there is also new potential if people work in a more interactive, conversational, and propositional way with smart systems. What if we treated smart systems as idiosyncratic colleagues rather than as conscripts?

"If the unforeseen is to become a resource, then digital objects ought to operate in ways that—in some circumstances—enable uncertainty rather than shun it or flatten it."—Betti Marenko and Phillip van Allen

HUMBLE ML/AI

ML/AI systems have significant limits, and are often not really that smart, so I call them "dumb-smart" due to their limited comprehension, narrow skills, and fallibility. This dumb-smartness can be leveraged and turned into an advantage by enabling people to interact simultaneously with multiple dumb systems that, together, are smarter.

Designing diverse ecologies with a humbler approach to ML/AI allows designers to move away from trying to provide single, correct answers. When there are multiple perspectives, "actually smart" humans can work out which threads to follow, make new connections, and give feedback to their evolving, hand-picked menagerie of risk-taking personalities.

Integrating human intelligence, selectivity, and discrimination into a multiplicitous ML/AI ecology makes ML/AI systems less brittle and able to tolerate errors more gracefully. And by embracing risk, unpredictability, and multiple points of view, there is an added benefit of an emergent, useful, and relevant serendipity.

TRANSPARENCY

Using animistic design, designers can telegraph point-of-view and limitations by giving smart devices appropriate personality behaviors. This can provide a much-needed transparency to the inner-workings of smart systems. Not a literal transparency, but a *curated, designed, metaphorical* transparency that's an interpretation of (often) inherently inscrutable ML/AI systems.

DISTRIBUTED COGNITION

The theory of distributed cognition recognizes that people don't only think inside their brain but extend their thinking into the environment through the things they interact with.

Their external milieu becomes an active thinking and creative medium: tangible, alive, and interactive. The mind arises within and through a person's milieu.

By assembling a tangible ecology of embodied animistic devices in a workspace, we allow people to leverage distributed cognition. One idea or concept can live here "in" *this* physical smart object, and another idea is over there "in" *that* smart object.

Through this physical embodiment, people can manipulate ideas in a spatial way, working *with* the ambiguous and diverse character of complex problems instead of *reducing* the complexity. Look at a typical design studio and you'll see the walls covered with different materials that stimulate the creative process. What if those things could have a conversation with you?

CONCLUSION

Animistic design proposes that smart digital entities adopt distinct personalities that inform their perceived sense of aliveness. Rather than having people work with a single, authoritative system, this approach has people engage with multiple smart systems, in which each entity has its own intentions, expertise, moods, goals, data sources, and methods. These are not, in my vision, cute anthropomorphic dolls. Instead, animistic design strives for a humble, more "native" digital animism, that embodies (metaphorically at least) the inherent affordances and limits of the computational/mechanical systems being developed.

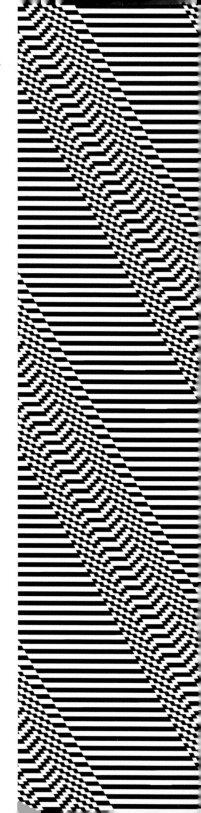

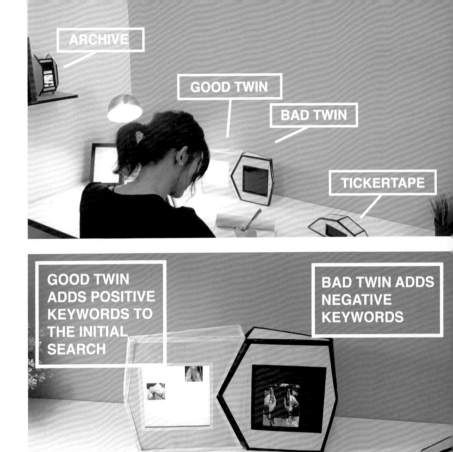

FIG 11. LITTLE DATA WRANGLERS. In this project, Philip van Allen reimagines the UX experience of ML/AI through the lens of animism. By generating a range of devices, each with its own distinct narrow intelligence and behavior, he facilitates a user experience that moves beyond the conscript model. Instead of interacting with one intelligence, the human user interacts with a milieu of intelligences. Van Allen explains, "I think it's dangerous to think of AI as being authoritative. The more the AI things around us differ, i.e., have different opinions and approaches, the more doubt humans will have about AI's authority. I think that's important."[1]

Machines Have Eyes

Anastasiia Raina, Lia Coleman, Meredith Binnette, Yimei Hu, Danlei Huang, Zack Davey, Qihang Li

Anastasiia Raina is a Ukrainian-born designer, researcher, and assistant professor at RISD (Rhode Island School of Design). Her research-based practice explores the aesthetics of technologically mediated nature through machine vision and evolutionary biology, incorporating biotechnology into the artistic vernacular. She draws upon scientific inquiry, working with scientists to generate new methodologies in design.

As artificial intelligence (AI) automates the aesthetic realm, we are surrounded by algorithms, and we function like them. From choosing typefaces to our next date, algorithms influence our senses and imagination by presenting carefully curated "truths" based on our previous selections and preferences. Machine-learning algorithms have become the artist, critic, dictator, and mediator of new realities. They present paintings at Art Basel, write the next Game of Thrones books, and curate exhibitions at the Tate. The idea that a computer can outdo humans in aesthetic pursuits—the prized attribute of humanness—presents an existential crisis, threatening the definition of what it means to be human.

We find ourselves in both a technological and philosophical paradigm shift that lies at the center of posthumanist discourse and calls for a reconsideration of technology, not as mere prosthesis but as integral to human identity and our process of technological coevolution. We should move beyond the conception of AI as an assistant or collaborator and begin to think about it as an extension of ourselves— a by-product of a quintessentially human quest to expand human abilities and better understand the world around us. By embedding posthumanist thought into our art and design practice, we address this crisis and emphasize the entangled nature of human and nonhuman systems, whether technological or biological.

EMERGENT NATURE OF FORM

Historically, humans have emulated living beings through imagination, storytelling, religion, science, and technology. For the past century, biomimicry has been integral in this emulation process, relying on the artist, designer, and engineer to study and copy the mechanisms found in Nature. By copying the behavior of the brain's neurons, the first neural network was developed—technology that can teach itself and improve over time with minimal to no human intervention.

Our planet has become a human design studio where we continue to copy and edit and reproduce Nature itself, participating in a continuous feedback loop between humans, technologies, and ecologies—which, in turn, reshape us and our cognition of what is natural and what is artificial. What does it mean to be inspired by Nature when we live in artificial and cyborg landscapes and ecosystems? What new design methodologies can we develop in this techno-ecology? The Posthuman Mobility Lab critically explored the process of nature simulation in art, design, and technology during a six-week RISD-Hyundai Summer Collaborative Research project. Five RISD graduate and undergraduate students from Industrial Design, Jewelry + Metalsmithing, Fine Arts, and Film/Animation/Video focused on one fascinating question: how is form generated when the boundary between the natural and the automated becomes obsolete?

We explored the evolutionary development process and environmental adaptation that results in unique capabilities and morphologies in plant, insect, and animal design. Our research employed style transfer and image synthesis capabilities of generative adversarial network (GAN) algorithms to analyze and combine the visual data into custom-generated models. We worked closely with AI researcher Lia Coleman, who introduced us to GAN algorithms and guided us through collecting a dataset, creating custom GAN models, and manipulating models in latent space. The process of training a StyleGAN model, generated images, and videos served as sources and material for our project, From Chaos to Order, a simulated environment that stimulates the growth and morphology of techno-ecological embryonic specimens.

SEEING AND HEARING THE INVISIBLE

In our research process, we found stark similarities between evolutionary development processes in Nature and neural networks—generating shape from a single cell into a whole organism, from noise to the pixel. The grainy GAN universe has no concept of time or sequence. It changes its appearance and color, continually replacing patterns of information with new layers, sculpting noise into embryo-like forms that emerge de novo in the first few hours of the GAN training process. Similarly, in evolutionary biology, all vertebrate embryos pass through a development stage where they appear somewhat similar. Embryos are microworlds, whose future topology is marked out by the evo-devo gene tool kit—a small subset of genes in an organism's genome that controls the organism's embryonic development.[1] Yet how do the tool kit genes know where to act and how to shape development? Or how does a GAN algorithm know where to place the pixels?

To survive and thrive, organisms and plants rely on sensing multiple environmental signals, such as gravity, light, or even touch. This phenomenon is known as tropism—organisms' response to directions and stimuli that trigger growth and shape change in plants and organisms.[2] Another phenomenon essential to organisms' growth is bioelectricity.[3] Along with genetic data, embryonic cells receive bioelectric cues that inform the initial development of structures such as cell type, tissue size, positional information, axial polarity, and organ identity.

Inspired by these two processes, we looked at the electrical noise as a source of stimuli and a force that connects us across species and landscapes, firing up our brains, bodies, fiber optic undersea cables, and servers as we speed through invisible internet infrastructures. Bringing insights from biology and information technology into the sphere of art, design, and sound, we activated variables in an audio-controlled environment to propagate the growth and morphology of a GAN-generated structure. In the resulting artificial environment, sound acts as growth stimuli: the 3D-coordinate of the sound source guides the general direction of growth; the amplitude of electronic sound and four-channel audios convert the shape and size; and noise fluctuations interfere with the degree of nonlinear distortion. Signaled by the environment, starting from digital noise to pixel, structures slowly grow and morph according to the surrounding sound changes.

FROM CHAOS TO ORDER

As artists and designers, we often think of AI-generated images as end points and are frustrated with generated blobbiness and a lack of technical understanding that prevents us from critically evaluating the images. The result is typically critiqued as a fault of GAN's fatal newness, raising philosophical questions of creativity, criticality, and ownership. The visual analysis fails when we look at an image generated by an invisible intelligence incomprehensible even to its engineers, who cannot explain operations inside the models by the sheer magnitude of parameters and dimensional input spaces. So how do artists and designers engage with this unintelligible intelligence?

By utilizing GAN algorithms in the visual research process, we can synthesize large, even humanly incomprehensible, amounts of visual data. Precisely with the help of our GAN model trained on over ten thousand images of insects and insect structures, we discovered formal coherence and underlying design principles in morphogenesis, helping us solidify our research focus.

The latent space itself becomes a space for contemplation and inspiration, where we begin to construct meaning and draw connections between forms composed of memories of images the model was initially trained on. Latent space in GAN algorithms consists of 512 dimensions. It serves as a representation of compressed data in which data points are scattered through space. Related data points are located in close proximity, producing infinite form variation and mutation of that specific image or shape. The generative aspect of the GAN algorithm gives a new dimension to visual methodology in art and design and provides practitioners with the ability to explore thousands of forms at once. We can iteratively develop different models that produce visually compelling results and optimize them based on feedback data. Furthermore, it equips us with the superhuman ability to recognize deep fakes and even predict the next image or frame!

As Posthuman Mobility Lab has set out to find new visual research methods of working with Nature systems and its technoscientific transformations, GAN algorithms have played a central role in our visual research, assisting us with visual analysis, inspiration, and form-making. Final generated forms are utterly alien to humans, both spatially and sequentially, because of hybrid intelligence collaboration. Nevertheless, these forms contain glimpses of genetic information of visual input data, delighting our minds with the challenge of catching sight of the familiar. The resulting deictic relationship between AI, animation, and sound composition is a direct by-product of human and nonhuman systems' entangled nature.

Our research demonstrates that we should look at AI-generated images, not as an end result, but as a process for engaging with and being inspired by the intelligence that has been programmed into them. By directly working with input data, modifying and intervening in the source code, we engage with an AI-generated image via its underlying algorithm, demystify this alien technology through direct interaction, and begin to gain agency over the process of techno-reductionism.

FIG 12. FROM ORDER TO CHAOS. How does form emerge when the boundary between the natural, artificial, and the automated becomes obsolete? From Chaos to Order is a research project that focused on developing techno-ecological design methodologies by integrating ML into visual research and design processes. As a result, the team developed a simulated audio environment that propagates the growth and morphology of embryonic specimens.

The project was developed by Anastasiia Raina, Lia Coleman, Meredith Binnette, Yimei Hu, Danlei Huang, Zack Davey, and Qihang Li, as part of the RISD-Hyundai–sponsored research partnership exploring the future of mobility.

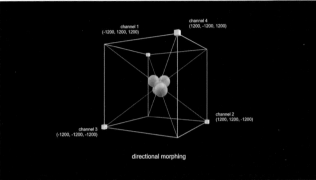

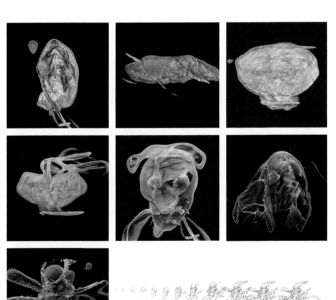

FIG 13. A MODEL TRAINED ON SEM (SEARCH ENGINE MARKETING) AND MICRO-CT SCANS OF INSECT ANATOMY. Generated StyleGan2 images were first sketched and later translated into 3D structures. Trained by Yimei Hu and Qihang Li.

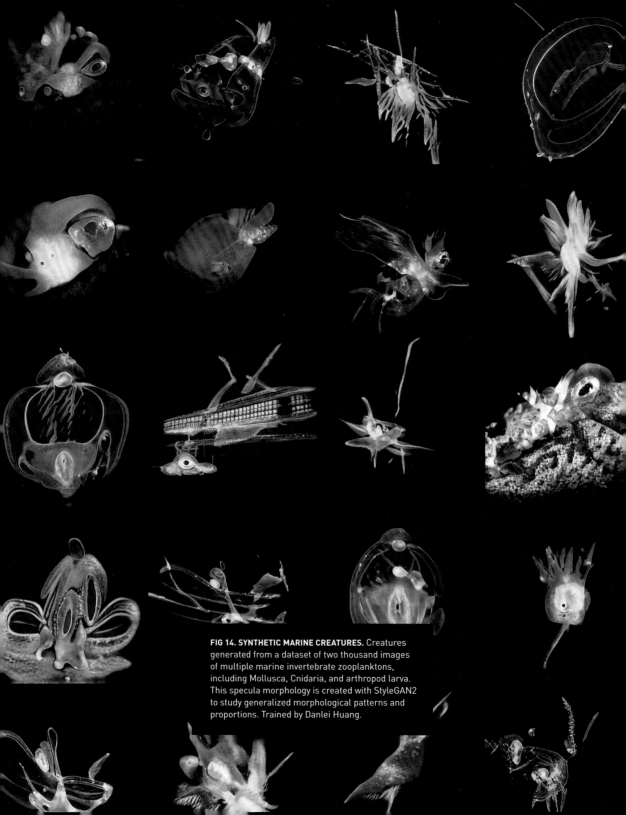

FIG 14. SYNTHETIC MARINE CREATURES. Creatures generated from a dataset of two thousand images of multiple marine invertebrate zooplanktons, including Mollusca, Cnidaria, and arthropod larva. This specula morphology is created with StyleGAN2 to study generalized morphological patterns and proportions. Trained by Danlei Huang.

CHAPTER TWO

Seize the Data

As machine learning (ML) propagates across multiple digital ecosystems, we are inviting computers into spaces that, for thousands of years, only humans have occupied. Our interactions with machines are shifting from "transactional" to "relational."[1] In essence, the static products of old—e.g., watches, speakers, ads, software platforms—are coming alive. As Silka Sietsma, head of Emerging Design at Adobe, asserts, our design practice now needs "to encompass not just the persona of a human [user] but also the personas of products—products that act like humans."[2] Designers will need to create interfaces that not only meet user needs but also can, themselves, learn, grow, and evolve over time. Before we design this next slew of products, we need to understand what happens when designers transfer human methods of interaction, such as language, emotional intelligence, and contextual awareness, to artificial systems.

"Machines with voices have particular power to make us feel understood."—Sherry Turkle, Massachusetts Institute of Technology

LET'S TALK

What should designers consider as they begin to dig into this new relational computer era? To understand, let's begin with a fundamental unit of human-to-human exchange: the conversation.[3] Using the ML-based technology natural language processing, computers can now analyze language to detect patterns between words, behaviors, and outcomes.[4] This heightened level of analysis and understanding enables computers to communicate with humans through conversational user interfaces (CUIs, i.e., natural language—think chatbots, virtual agents like Alexa or Siri, or any other voice- or text-based interface. A CUI can identify a user and instantly individualize to meet their needs: "Hello, Susan, should I call your daughter and tell her you will be late?" A CUI can also bridge devices, rising above disparate devices to provide immediate access. It can even follow you from location to location—your house, your car, a hotel room—so that you can pick up and resume conversations that you began a day or a month ago.[5] But our attraction to conversational interfaces goes beyond individualization and access.

A growing number of people talk with chatbots and more sophisticated virtual agents. In 2019, Woebot Health's chatbot Woebot was exchanging nearly 3 million conversations with users a week, and Amazon had sold 100 million Alexa devices.[6] [Fig. 8] In 2020, hundreds of thousands of people were each sending around seventy messages daily to Replika, a personal artificial intelligence (AI) companion.[7] [Fig. 16] Microsoft Xiaoice, a popular social chatbot designed to form long-term emotional connections with users, has over 660 million users, primarily in China.[8] In response to the COVID-19 pandemic, the Centers for Disease Control and Prevention (CDC) and the World Health Organization (WHO) both created

NATURAL LANGUAGE PROCESSING: a branch of AI that focuses on how computers analyze, process, and generate human language

CONVERSATIONAL USER INTERFACE (CUI): a user interface with a computer that imitates the back-and-forth conversational style of humans

CHATBOT: software application that uses AI and natural language processing to engage in conversations with humans

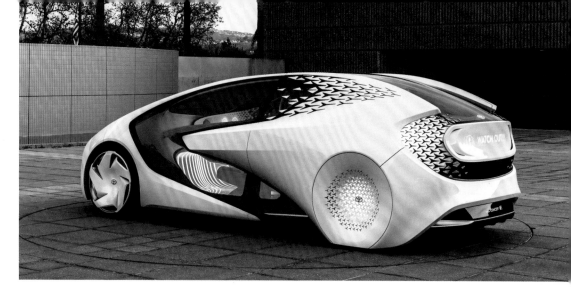

FIG 15. CONCEPT-I. Design and technology studio Tellart worked with Toyota's Advanced Design team to create the user experience for this emotionally intelligent autonomous concept car. Through this work, Tellart delves into the warm relationships we might form with objects that can get to know us over time.

FIG 16. REPLIKA. Created by Luka, a startup founded by Eugenia Kuyda, this virtual agent chats with an individual intensely over time, learning from their speech patterns so that it might create a "replika"—a virtual copy. Kuyda got the idea for the agent when she trained a neural network to replicate the texting patterns of a close friend who died in a tragic accident. Kuyda looks to a day when a digital representation of you could go out into the world and take care of all the things you don't want to deal with.[9]

FIG 17. SAMSUNG NATURAL GESTURE. Josh Clark's team at Big Medium worked with Samsung to prototype a hand gesture system. Users wearing a smart-watch could use the resulting natural gestures to interact with their phones more intuitively.

chatbots to disseminate information efficiently, offer emotional support, and advise actions.[10] Why have conversational interfaces become so popular? What's so different about using natural language to communicate with a computer? How does conversing with a machine differ from typing, clicking, scrolling, or touching a graphical user interface (GUI)? Why have conversational interfaces proven so likeable—even lovable?

Over thousands of years, humans have evolved to respond to anyone or anything speaking as they would to a human being. According to researchers Clifford Nass and Scott Brave, "listeners and talkers cannot suppress their natural responses to speech regardless of source." Even if a computer voice is purposefully constructed to sound artificial, humans will treat the "voice with the same social assumptions and behaviors as a biological voice."[11] Think about all the evolutionary and cultural baggage that you bring to each conversation with another person. Humans now bring those same understandings into our conversations with machines.

What do designers need to know about this human phenomenon? In the first few minutes of a conversation, humans assign gender to a voice—along with all current gender biases and stereotypes. We also quickly assign personality to the voice and make personality judgments. And those judgments tend to stick with us, flavoring subsequent interactions. Just as with another human, we will have a tendency to like the virtual personality that is most similar to our own—the principle of "similarity attraction." In addition, humans will distrust a personality that demonstrates inconsistency, the Stroop Effect. And before you think you could never fall for the spell of a synthetic voice, guess what? You will. It's built into human DNA, including yours. Nass and Brave point out that participants in their studies consistently demonstrated this behavior, all the while confidently decrying such a human reaction to a synthetic voice.[12]

Designers creating interfaces that engage with speech are producing complex social interactions whether they intend to or not. It's easy to see how complexities might permeate

GRAPHICAL USER INTERFACE (GUI): an interface through which users interact with electronic devices via visual representations

SYNTHETIC VOICE: artificial production of human speech

"We use words to find our way. Alexa can only help us get to a place we already know we want to go. Not help us grow."—Paul Pangaro, Carnegie Mellon University

a user's relationship with an intelligent interface or digital product. Is the user attracted to a product's personality? Does an individual distrust the product's erratic behavior? Do human stereotypes come into play?

Let's dig deeper into the nature of conversation and its potential for leveraging relational interactions with technology. What is a conversation anyway? Paul Pangaro, a design professor at Carnegie Mellon University, studies conversation as interaction. He looks to cybernetician Gordon Pask for a humanistic perspective, an understanding of the nature of human interchange. Pangaro notes that, in essence, each participant in a conversation forms their own goal for engaging and then a back and forth ensues. The exchange leads to an agreement of goals and, ultimately, a coordinated action.[13]

As designers imbue their products with personality and speech, what high-impact conversational terrain could emerge? Pangaro observes: "Today's interfaces are not bad at coordination. Turn on the light. What's the temperature? How many people live in Philadelphia? These are informational. Or, buy me more dish soap. This is transactional—the origin of Amazon's interest in Alexa. These interfaces coordinate action, but they don't allow a sophisticated kind of cooperation or collaboration."[14]

Instead of focusing simply on coordination and transaction, Pangaro asserts, designers should explore conversational situations in which participants enter the experience without certainty, unsure of both the goal and how to get there. For example, think back to the last conversation with a friend or partner that started with a question like, "What should we accomplish this year?" The conversation that might ensue from an open-ended query like this can propel participants into unknown territory; unforeseen possibilities can emerge. According to Pangaro, through such a rich conversational

FIG 18. NICO, CLEANING ASSISTANT. In this prototype, visually impaired users interact with intelligent glasses to detect and clean spills in their kitchens. The eyeglasses use image recognition to isolate spills while conversing with the user privately via bone conduction to assist them with cleanup. The familiar format—eyeglasses—allows users to scan their spaces using natural gestures. Designed by North Carolina State University MGD students: Ellis Anderson, Alyssa Buchanan, Matt Babb.

FIG 19. ELIZA. Joseph Weizenbaum created this oft-cited general conversational program in the 1960s, naming it after Eliza from George Bernard Shaw's play *Pygmalion.* Weizenbaum was upset when people suggested that the chatbot be used as an actual therapist. He warns, "Ultimately a line dividing human and machine intelligence must be drawn. If there is no such line, then advocates of computerized psychotherapy may be merely heralds of an age in which man has finally been recognized as nothing but a clock-work."[15]

interface space participants could begin to collaborate with intelligent systems to "tame wicked problems," the high-consequence issues of our time, such as hunger, sustainability, disease; and racial inequity.[16]

WAIT, BUT HOW ARE YOU FEELING?

Conversation is one area for designers to keep an eye on as they work with ML to develop intelligent products. What else? What other paths lead to richer collaborative relationships with machine intelligence? As AI researcher Subbarao Kambhampati asserts, one path lies in nurturing AI's social, emotional intelligence. Cognitive intelligence, he maintains, is not enough. Humans are social, emotional creatures. To effectively interface with a human, computers must exhibit appropriate emotional behavior.[17]

Kambhampati uses Microsoft's Clippy, first released in 1997, as an example. People hated Clippy, a cartoony paperclip with eyes, because the emotional reaction was off—perpetually peppy and smug. Interacting with a machine with limited or incongruous social and emotional responses exhausts users.[18] Sietsma explains, "The standard for good design has risen. An autonomous product cannot just reflect us but [must] have an understanding of the effect it has on us…. Computers now need to not just build empathy, but to also show empathy."[19]

Designer Steph Hay asserts a similar idea based on her work with Capital One's virtual assistant, Eno. She advises, "When designing for AI, embrace emotion. Use emotion as a design material to establish trust [because] trust drives behavioral change for both sides, the end user and the designer."[20] If we do not focus on creating machines with an adroit social, emotional intelligence, we will bypass a future of humans and computers living and collaborating together. Instead, as Kambhampati warns, we will end up with computers that don't understand us—and don't need us. We will be "designing our own obsolescence."[21]

WICKED PROBLEM: social or cultural problem that is difficult or impossible to solve

END USER: person who ultimately uses or is intended to use a product

DEEP LEARNING: based loosely on the human brain, this ML system filters information hierarchically through hidden layers—artificial neural networks; it's capable of learning unsupervised from unstructured data

"What is the value of interaction that contains no shared experience of life and contributes nothing to a shared store of human meaning—and indeed may devalue it?"
—Sherry Turkle, Massachusetts Institute of Technology

Certainly, we don't want to design away human usefulness. Appropriate social, emotional responses by AI, it seems, could help bridge the human machine divide, keeping humans in play. As absurd as it sounds, humans and machines do have to get along. But does it matter that computers can't actually feel anything? That the whole emotional dance is a big fat lie?

DOES IT MATTER THAT IT'S A LIE?

In 1964, Joseph Weizenbaum created an early natural language processing computer program, ELIZA, at the MIT Artificial Intelligence Laboratory. Rather than the deep learning methods of today, this early chatbot used simple pattern matching to simulate conversational responses to a user. In the most famous interaction script, DOCTOR, the chatbot, simulated a Rogerian psychotherapist. [Fig. 19] Weizenbaum was alarmed to find a number of people treated ELIZA like a living entity, sharing intimate secrets. In response, he urged that we differentiate between *deciding* and *choosing* in the technology we make. A computer, he admonished, should only decide, i.e., use logic to make a calculation. It shouldn't appear to choose because choice, according to Weizenbaum, requires human capabilities like compassion and wisdom. Simulating choice by a machine was a lie—a lie that troubled Weizenbaum.[22]

Does this "lie" matter? ML tech is making it more likely that a machine's ability to read and respond to our emotions will improve. Patents give some indication of the future. Amazon has patented technology to enable Alexa to monitor users' emotions, analyzing the pitch and volume of speaker commands, and respond according to how they're "feeling." Google and IBM have developed similar patents. IBM's patent specifically references the scrutiny of facial recognition, heart

FIG 20. AIMOJI. Process Studio (Martin Grödl, Moritz Resl) created these AI-generated emojis for the Vienna Biennale for Change 2019, using a Deep Convolutional Generative Adversarial Network (DCGAN). According to the studio, "with each Almoji, new, hitherto unknown 'artificial' emotions come to life that challenge us to interpret and interact with them." The Almojis underpinned Process Studio's identity work for the exhibition *UNCANNY VALUES. Artificial Intelligence & You* at MAK—Museum of Applied Arts, Vienna, curated by Paul Feigelfeld and Marlies Wirth. For more information: www.process.studio.[23]

rate, and even brain waves.[24] Despite controversy around the validity of facial expressions as emotional indicators, such patents suggest a variety of strategies could be used in concert to increase accuracy.[25] What issues will emerge as emotional analysis techniques improve? If the response is appropriate, does it matter it's coming from an AI?

MIT professor Sherry Turkle, in her book *Reclaiming Conversation*, questions, "Who do we become when we talk to machines?" She argues that interacting with virtual agents can't teach us about real relationships because machines can't truly feel or empathize. By interacting with machines, we forget what it means to be human, to be intimate. Turkle warns, "Even as we treat machines as if they were almost human, we develop habits that have us treating human beings as almost-machines." The machines, in essence, will train us. What are the psychological implications of designing intelligent interfaces that encourage humans to bond with machines that can only simulate emotional responses?[26]

Historian Yuval Noah Harari carries this idea further. The machines won't turn against us or consider us irrelevant. Instead, he warns, we might prefer them over other humans: "One scenario is that if AI becomes better at understanding our feelings and emotions we may become intolerant of humans because they are less empathetic than the computers."[27]

Let's step back from this rather stark vision for a moment. If social, emotional intelligence proves crucial for future human-computer relations, perhaps designers should begin to consider in what contexts such emotional intelligence might or might not be appropriate—rather than writing it off entirely. When should designers encourage emotional bonding with AI and when should they actively discourage it?

CAN AN AI MAKE YOU MORE EMPATHETIC?

Kate Darling's work is useful to consider here. Darling, a research specialist at the MIT Media Lab, considers the effects of encouraging or discouraging people to anthropomorphize

ANTHROPOMORPHIZE: attributing human characteristics or behavior to nonhuman entities.

> **"What happens when your refrigerator is more attuned to your emotions than your husband is?"**
> —Yuval Noah Harari, Hebrew University of Jerusalem

intelligent products, specifically robots. Humans have a long history of applying human emotions and behavior to nonhuman things. Remember the stuffed octopus that you spoke to as a child? The car you patted on the dash to make it up a steep hill? The Wi-Fi you named and cursed when it cut out?

Ultimately, Darling finds that anthropomorphic framing—a name, a personality, a backstory, a biological form—can be useful if such framing fits with the product's underlying functionality. For example, as she notes, simply shipping a medicine delivery robot with an individual name can result in friendlier attitudes and a higher tolerance level by hospital staff. However, in some contexts, anthropomorphic framing can cause undue stress in human users. For instance: "One robot was built to walk on and detonate landmines. The colonel overseeing the testing exercise for the machine ended up stopping it because the sight of the robot dragging itself along the minefield was too 'inhumane' to bear." In this context, encouraging users to relate to the digital product—the robot—as a fellow human prevented it from completing its task effectively.

SOCIAL SCIENCE: the branch of science devoted to the relationships among individuals within societies

Darling goes on to suggest that encouraging empathetic relationships with AI, rather than weakening our human-to-human connections, might instead strengthen them. Her research finds that it's possible to measure people's empathy by observing their interactions with lifelike robots. Based on these findings, she posits that the opposite might also be true: we might be able to leverage human empathy toward nonliving things to promote better treatment of other humans.[28] [Fig. 22]

As theorists like Turkle, Harari, and Darling demonstrate, the closer we move to intelligent interfaces and products, the more complex the terrain of the designer and the more the expertise of social scientists becomes part of the equation. As machine-generated detection and expression of language and emotion encourage deeper connections between human and machine, novel, complex design challenges will emerge. And relationships, after all, can be fraught.

SYMBIOSIS, PLEASE

What other difficulties will surface as our relationship with intelligent interfaces tightens? In addition to building relationships *between* humans and machines, could designers begin to mix human and nonhuman intelligences together as ML improves? Could designers leverage the strengths of both entities to develop previously unattainable or unimaginable capabilities—all with a wider cultural impact in mind?

Merging human and machine intelligences, or "symbiosis," is not a new concept. J. C. R. Licklider wrote in 1960 in his influential article, "Man-Computer Symbiosis": "The hope is that, in not too many years, human brains and computing machines will be coupled together very tightly, and that resulting partnership will think as no human brain has ever thought and process data in a way not approached by the information-handling machines we know today."[29] Humans have been moving toward symbiosis for quite some time.

Human + Machine = Centaur

WOULD YOU LIKE TO BE A "CENTAUR?"

What's a centaur? In 1998, a year after being defeated in chess by IBM's Deep Blue, chess champion Garry Kasparov played on a human/AI team. Rather than pitting human and AI against one another, this scenario tried to produce the strongest combined player by bringing the entities together. The model of the centaur emerged: part human, part machine intelligence, one entity. In a later chess tournament in 2005, the centaur succeeded in winning—a human/AI team beat both solo humans and solo computers.[30] We still hear this term used today referencing combined human–machine intelligence.

INTEGRATION, *NOT INTERACTION*

In 2016, Umer Farooq and Jonathan Grudin of Microsoft built upon this centaur idea as they asserted humans are transitioning into a period of "human-computer *integration*."[31] Interaction, they maintain, suggests a stimulus-response model: the user asks the computer to do something and it complies. The computer then sits, waiting, for the user's next request. In contrast, "integration" suggests more of a partnership; both the human and the machine have a degree of autonomy as they work together toward goals.

Farooq and Grudin's integration model expands the designer's consideration from what happens when a human makes requests of a computer to what the computer *might also do* when users *are not* directing requests. In other words, what *could* the computer do when the user is not interacting with it? How might this affect the user experience?

Our earlier discussion around anticipatory design begins to address this question. Machine-learning algorithms might be gathering and analyzing data behind the scenes to provide a frictionless, individualized user experience. But we can also look at this from a different perspective: as humans and computers blur together, the resulting feedback loops could harness the strengths of both to serve multiple goals for multiple parties.

FEEDBACK LOOP: part of a system in which all of or a portion of a system's output is used as input for future operations

THE FEEDBACK LOOP

Patrick Hebron, Adobe's Machine Intelligence Design team lead, uses the ReCAPTCHA system to explain the value of symbiotic machine relationships to designers via the intelligent feedback loop. Originally, the CAPTCHA system verified that a system user was human by asking the user to complete a small task that would be difficult for a machine. The functionality ended when the user was granted or denied entry to a site. Researchers at Carnegie Mellon University designed a new system, the ReCAPTCHA, that turned this process into a feedback loop that benefits both human user and AI.[32]

FIG 21. BEEBOP. This ironic virtual agent, prototyped by North Carolina State University graduate student Jessye Holmgren-Sidell, trains users to address it properly by manipulating their emotions. If users speak to the agent improperly, the agent experiences physical pain—blackened eyes or sliced-off arms and legs. To stop the pain, users must learn the right way to phrase requests.

FIG 22. HARMING AND PROTECTING ROBOTS: CAN WE? SHOULD WE? MIT Media Lab research specialist Kate Darling led a workshop in which she asked participants to torture and kill a robotic dinosaur with a hammer after naming it and interacting with it. Participants refused to hit the dinosaurs. Darling suggests that the way we treat machines can be indicative of how we treat other humans. In other words, we may be able to "measure people's empathy using robots."[33]

In ReCAPTCHA, the system learns from the results of each human task, feeding the knowledge back to the AI tech to improve it. Google acquired the ReCAPTCHA technology, and many of us have experienced the results. We enter a website and then are required to verify that we are humans by completing a task. For example, after viewing a grid of images, we might be asked to select a category of objects—all the stoplights, all the crosswalks, etc. The results serve two purposes: 1) it determines whether the user is really a human for the website in question, and 2) it uses our choices to improve Google's image recognition technology for autonomous cars.

Systems like these raise interesting possibilities. How can designers create systems in which humans and machines learn from each other in recursive loops? How can the interface you are designing not just respond to immediate user needs but recognize and utilize the unique capabilities of humans and of machine cognition? How might the resulting system serve not just the user but also other stakeholders—overtly or covertly. And should the user have some say in who those other stakeholders are? "Who does Alexa work for anyway—you, Amazon, countless others?"[34]

We will return to questions of ML transparency and user control in chapter three when we dig more into how designers might reveal what machine intelligences are doing beyond the user's awareness. For now, let's continue to consider how to leverage the strength of human and machine together to create new capabilities and better user experiences. Let's start with context.

RECURSIVE LOOP: when a function or model makes calls to itself repeatedly, thus forming an almost infinite loop

STAKEHOLDERS: people with an interest or concern in an entity, like a business

WHAT CONTEXT?

Devices today are not really aware of context, i.e., what is happening outside of the device. Knowing about context will allow devices to be more proactive in helping people, supplying relevant information that will allow people to be "in the moment, more focused on the current task" rather than switching gears to respond to devices that constantly interrupt

"Cognitive enhancement: systems that seamlessly enhance aspects of cognition to help the user become (or remain) the person they want to be."—Pattie Maes, Massachusetts Institute of Technology

not just us but also one another.[35] Imagine, for example, that you are running in a marathon. An AI could intervene when you are slowing at a crucial moment in the race. At the same time, the AI could block all irrelevant incoming texts and phone calls.

This understanding of context, or external states, in MIT professor Pattie Maes's research, is not just about fitting a task into the appropriate moment in a series of actions. Her group, Media Lab Fluid Interfaces Group, investigates how devices might engage sensors to combine external data with a user's internal data to sharpen and expand an individual's cognition: a goal she terms "cognitive enhancement."[36]

For example, AttentivU, developed by Nataliya Kos'myna and Maes, takes on a human's ability to focus, an issue for 10 percent of kids today. In this device prototype, eyeglasses provide gentle audio or haptic feedback when electrooculography (EOG) electrodes detect an individual's drop in engagement, thus redirecting participants when their attention wanders.[37] [Fig. 23] Another Fluid Interfaces project, BioEssence, reads the physiology of the user and then delivers real-time olfactory interventions in response to stress, anxiety, or depressive symptoms.[38] [Fig. 24] Through ML tech, the device monitors the user to improve effective intervention, while simultaneously, the user becomes more aware of their own internal state and outward responses. Human and machine draw from context to work symbiotically and thus build insight in both entities. Designers can easily see the user benefits of generating such systems—less disruptive tech interventions, reduced cognitive load, frictionless in-the-moment responses, and successful task completion. But might there also be drawbacks?

DEPENDENCE: A DETRIMENT?

The word *symbiosis* conveys interdependence. When designers begin to construct symbiotic relationships between humans and machines, both sides of this relationship come into play—*what people gain but also what they lose.* Much has been written in recent years questioning human's growing dependence on technology and the resulting erosion of skills. We hear of pilots forgetting how to fly because of autopilot, doctors forgetting basic operating skills, people losing their navigational skills as a result of GPS systems.[39] Each time a design team opts to add features that shift a skill from a human to a device, known as "deskilling," they face a decision with wide social implications. Sure, the product might decrease cognitive load and improve the efficiency of task completion, but what are humans losing in the process?[40]

TECHNO-DETERMINISM: a reductionist theory that proposes that technology in any given society defines its nature

If we carry this line of thinking forward, might humans eventually shift their decision-making process entirely over to machines, losing the ability to make crucial choices? After all, who loves to make hard decisions? Harari warns: "Once AI makes better decisions than we do about careers and perhaps even relationships, our concept of humanity and of life will have to change. Humans are used to thinking about life as a drama of decision-making."[41] Harari sees this shift ultimately as a challenge to liberal democracy, a political ideology based on individual autonomy and agency.

Let's resist throwing up our hands and succumbing to techno-determinism, however. Although quite compelling, Harari's vision represents only one possible future. Designers can create interfaces that take skills away, but they can also design systems that purposefully preserve or even build skills. As Maes explains, "A GPS system could be built differently. It could still know the right answer, but maybe it could ask us, 'Do you think you should go right or left here?'…And then if you answer incorrectly, it could tell you. No, actually, it's left. It could be designed….[to] force the person to think about and develop that task internally."[42] Rather than just automate existing skills, an intelligent system might strengthen or

FIG 23. ATTENTIVU. This device monitors brain activity and eye movements to measure cognitive processes in real time. When the device detects a specific user state—such as inattention—the system can provide gentle haptic or audio feedback to the user. Careful to preserve user privacy around data, the eyeglasses function in a non-networked system. Designed by MIT Fluid Interface Group: Pattie Maes and Nataliya Kos'myna.

FIG 24. BIOESSENCE. A wearable olfactory display, this device releases scents based on the wearer's physiological state. Users can map physiological conditions to different scents via a smartphone app to customize the experience. Designed by MIT Fluid Interface Group: Pattie Maes, Judith Amores Fernandez, Artem Dementyev, Javier Hernandez.

FIG 25. NEVERMIND. This device strengthens human memory by combining memory palace memorization methods with augmented reality (AR). Users can customize the experience by curating their own list of items to remember and then pairing that list with a familiar physical route. Using the AR tech the content is then overlaid on the route as the user moves through space. Designed by MIT Fluid Interface Group: Pattie Maes, Oscar Rosello, Marc Exposito Gomez.

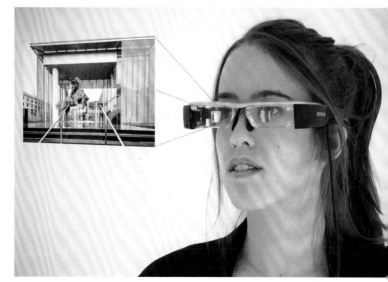

FIG 26. NORAA (MACHINIC DOODLES). Designer Jessica In created this live drawing installation in which a robot—NORAA—collaborates with a human. As In explains, it is "essentially a game of human-robot Pictionary: you draw, the machine takes a guess, and then draws something back in response." The ML system encodes each drawing through movement and sequence rather than image recognition. In notes that such systems not only explore collaborative creative processes with AI but can also reveal patterns in how people around the world draw, bringing new insight to the human drawing process.[43]

FIG 27. DEBUILD.CO. This tool allows users to generate the code for a fully functioning app by just describing it to OpenAI's new language generator GPT-3. This project, spearheaded by computer scientist Sharif Shameem, looks to a day when designers can use natural language to communicate with a computer. In other words, creatives will be able to design by describing what they want rather than manipulating mouse clicks, menu items, and code.

debuild.co

Describe your app.   Clear   Generate   Add $3   Withdraw $5

a button that says "Add $3" and a
button that says "Withdraw $5" and a
button that says "Give away all my
money". then show me my balance

Give away all my money

My balance is 0

```
// a button that says "Add $3" and
a button that says "Withdraw $5"
and a button that says "Give away
all my money". then show me my
balance
class App extends React.Component
```

Skills to Keep   VS.   Skills to Automate

improve inherent human skills, like memory, focus, empathy, etc. For example, in the Fluid Interfaces project NeverMind, developed by Oscar Rosello, Marc Exposito Gomez, and Maes, augmented reality (AR) glasses help strengthen an individual's memory skills using an ancient technique called the "memory palace." Individuals walk a familiar physical path while the AR glasses superimpose specific content on landmarks along the way. Later, without the glasses, the user can remember the content by associating words with their spatial memory. The system strengthens rather than replaces the user's innate memory.[44] [Fig. 25]

AGENCY: capacity of individuals to act independently and make their own free choices

In this way, AI helps individuals grow stronger and thrive even when automated systems aren't there. As designer Sarah Gold, founder of the technology studio IF emphasizes: "As we found in the pandemic working from home, tech fails all the time....How do we help people not feel helpless when automated systems fail?...How can designers help people maintain or increase their agency even as we automate parts of their lives?"[45] Suddenly, designers find themselves delineating what humans can and cannot do—which skills are strengthened and which are diminished—by including or excluding specific features in intelligent interfaces or products.

ARE YOU SCARED?

Should designers be frightened by the weight of these decisions? Be frightened. Now more than ever, data scientists and developers need designers on their teams as the guardians of human experience. We, in turn, need to consult with cognition experts. Coders can code, but designers will design humanity into ML. We need to think long and hard about what form this humanity will take as we couple closely with machines.

Such high-impact design decisions are incredibly difficult to make. To avoid a future defined by what's technically possible rather than what's preferable, researchers suggest we need to incorporate human-centered long-term thinking at the forefront of our projects, possibly through systems design methodologies. Sietsma, for example, suggests back casting, i.e., determine all the possible futures and then work backward to negate the bad ones while encouraging the good ones.[46] This methodology fits within a metastrategy in which we ask ourselves, "What kind of world do we want and then how can we design technologies to serve that vision rather than driving it?"[47]

ARTICULATING THE HUMAN

Beatriz Colomina and Mark Wigley, in their book, *Are We Human?*, assert that it is the vagueness of what constitutes the human that incites us to design: "If the human is a question mark, *design* is a word for how that question is engaged. Design literally takes shape, makes shape, through the indeterminacy of the human. Or, to say it the other way around, there would be no concept of design if the human was something clear and stable."[48] Over the last thirty years, designers have struggled quite rigorously to delineate the human by articulating human users and human needs as a core impetus for their practice. Human-centered design (HCD) methods have reshaped human computer interaction, interaction design, experience design, and a range of other design-oriented disciplines since the 1980s.[49]

Building symbiotic relationships with machines broadens HCD to include other players and concerns.[50] Now more than ever, humans do not stand at the center of the design process alone. As Anastasiia Raina, a multidisciplinary design professor at the Rhode Island School of Design (RISD), notes, "Introducing the term *collaboration* into our work with nonhuman

"How do we develop alien knowledge and alien thinking to have greater agency in the midst of this tectonic shift that is shaping our lives?"—Anastasiia Raina, Rhode Island School of Design

THE
SERVICE DOG
◆

If your product was entirely dedicated to empowering the lives of an underserved population, what kind of impact could you make?

Who could your product most directly benefit outside of your targeted users?

How would your product change to better serve them?

THE
SERVICE DOG

THE
SIREN

THE
SIREN
◆

What would using your product "too much" look like?

How does your product encourage users to engage, and how does it make it easy to disconnect?

How does your product respect people's boundaries and the other parts of their lives?

In what situations might it be inappropriate or distracting to use your product?

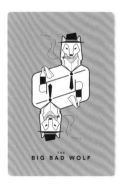

THE
BIG BAD WOLF

THE
BIG BAD WOLF
◆

What could a bad actor do with your product?

What would predatory and exploitative behavior look like with your product?

What product features are most vulnerable to manipulation?

Who could be targeted with your product?

FIG 28. TAROT CARDS OF TECH. Designers at Artefact generated this tool to help creators envision positive opportunities for change around technology. The cards encourage people to use a human-centered approach to query possible futures from a range of perspectives, such as "The Siren: What would using your product 'too much' look like?" or "The Radio Star: Who or what disappears if your product is successful?" or "Mother Nature: If the environment was your client, how would your product change?"

entities is a provocation, which compels us to acknowledge their agency and personhood."[51] We need to build upon the knowledge hard earned through HCD to augment our approaches with design methods better suited to the symbiotic human-AI paradigm.

Other disciplines like science and technology studies, social sciences, and the humanities can provide designers with some alternatives that can complement and expand traditional human-centered approaches.[52] Actor-network theory, distributed cognition, cybernetics, new materialism, and posthumanism all place humans as part of a much larger system that includes nonhumans. In essence, rather than working to stridently view our projects primarily through the perspective of potential human users, these approaches give designers more of a bird's-eye view or shift the viewpoint to that of a nonhuman entity, helping us to reposition users— and ourselves—within complex systems. As noted by design researchers Carl DiSalvo and Jonathan Lukens, in such perspectives "the human is not negated, because frequently… a non-anthropocentric perspective often is a means to an end of some human benefit."[53] In other words, all things are connected. Looking beyond the human does not necessarily mean positioning oneself in opposition to human interests and values.

Superflux creative director Anab Jain, reflects a similar perspective when she calls for "a 'more-than-human' centered approach. Where human beings are not at the center of the universe and the center of everything. Where we consider ourselves as deeply entangled in relationships with other species and nonhuman entities."[54] In his essay "The Enlightenment is Dead, Long Live the Entanglement," Danny Hillis warns us, "We can no longer understand how the world works by breaking it down into loosely-connected parts that reflect the hierarchy of physical space or deliberate design. Instead, we must watch the flows of information, ideas, energy, and matter

ACTOR-NETWORK THEORY: a sociological theory for understanding humans and their interactions with inanimate objects by suggesting relationships in the social and natural worlds exist in constantly shifting networks

DISTRIBUTED COGNITION: a learning framework that proposes cognition and knowledge are not restricted to an individual; rather, it is distributed across objects, individuals, artifacts, and tools in the environment—i.e., an extended mind

CYBERNETICS: "the science of communications and control systems in machines and living entities" —Norbert Wiener, 1948

NEW MATERIALISM: in resistance to modern and humanist traditions, this theoretical approach questions the stability of the individual subject and repositions humans among nonhuman actants while emphasizing the materiality of the world and everything— social and natural— within it

POSTHUMANISM: a theoretical approach that questions historical notions of the human, such as human subjectivity and embodiment

"I strongly believe that it is very important to play with these ideas scientifically and explore applications of machine intelligence that totter between being unimaginably oppressive and unbelievably exciting."
—Nicholas Negroponte, Massachusetts Institute of Technology

that connect us, and the networks of communication, trust, and distribution that enable these flows."[55] As designers grapple with the blending of human and machine, we will be forced to develop new theories and methods to define this emerging entangled world.

IN SUM: WE'VE GOT COMPANY

If we want a future in which humans and machines work together to move our society forward, we will have to design intelligent products that support thriving human-computer relationships. Language and emotions provide one avenue for more natural, intuitive user experiences, but they also raise questions around how these budding experiences will seep back into our connections to other humans. Integrated models of symbiosis suggest that we can leverage human and machine cognition, embracing the strengths of both to create recursive feedback loops. To do this, however, computers need to be able to detect patterns from both internal and external human activities—i.e., context. We've got to be careful, though, because creating tight interdependent relationships with AI could lead to the deskilling of humans. Designers have to be purposeful in how we build systems that shift abilities over to machines rather than haphazardly responding to market desires. Designers are, in essence, formulating and reformulating what it means to be human as they support or take away inherent human skills and abilities. We are going to need new design methods that move beyond human-centered design as our relationships with machines thicken. We no longer stand alone at the center of the design process.

SILKA SIETSMA
Interview

As head of emerging design at Adobe, Silka Sietsma focuses on the future of immersive design and AI-related products and services. Prior to Adobe, she led the AR (augmented reality) design direction for a Samsung innovation team and cofounded and led the product design for AR startup Dekko.

Can you speak about the relationship between design and technology?

Being head of emerging design at Adobe doesn't mean that I'm in love with technology. In fact, I feel very neutral about it in the same way you might feel neutral about a hammer. It is a tool. It is a tool that we give human qualities. Artificial intelligence is different in that it can also exhibit human qualities. In 2016, I started to see, through our elections, the effect that AI has on our society. That's when I started talking about the need for designers to think about not just how products can build empathy in users but also show empathy. The standard for good design rises when an autonomous product does not just reflect us but is able to have an understanding of the effect it has on us.

Artificial intelligence powers spatial computing, the next computing platform. Spatial computing will mesh digital experiences with physical reality through AR and VR (virtual reality), voice, and embedded sensors. Humans naturally interact with the world through our senses. If we are designing for spatial computing, we are, in essence, designing for human perception. We take information into our senses, our brain processes it, then our memories get put into that. We come out with what we understand is reality, our sense of truth. This is a huge current shift in design. Designers have the power to affect what you perceive is reality. And that is very, very scary. And if designers aren't scared, that makes me more scared. But it also gives me a sense of brave hope in how we are thinking about it now. I put together a group of people who are cognitive scientists and engineers and designers and machine-learning experts. And we started trying to create frameworks for designing for spatial computing using a combination of machine sensors and our human senses—all powered by artificial intelligence.

I am an optimist. The point of all this effort is, I hope, that we stop hiding behind screens. We can anticipate problems with artificial intelligence. But, we can also draw a little closer together using remote communication if we experience that communication more naturally.

Have you had experiences with designers who have really struggled to implement these ideas and tools?
People think this is all happening right now. We've reached general intelligence today. It's not. We are still at the beginning of artificial intelligence. It's clunky. It's narrow in what it can do. We're building up our understanding of the boundaries and the guidelines. People are struggling because they want to do more. But there's not enough yet developed to make a whole lot of fundamental changes. Everyone's so keen and willing to ask the hard questions and go through it. We want to do more, but we can't because it's still early days. Which is ironic.

A strength of artificial intelligence is that it can provide services that are specific to your needs—unique to the way that you express yourself. If I want to work a certain way, if the tool understands and learns how I'm working, then the tool can shift rather than me shifting around its static sensibilities. It can take on my personality. It could work with people who have dyslexia, like myself, or who may not be able to see some colors or may have other disabilities with sight, hearing, touch, communication. Tools can gear toward everybody—because we all have certain strengths and weaknesses. I like to think about tools being able to morph that way.

I also like to think about our tools becoming less dominant and our creativity becoming more dominant. I enjoy being able to pick up a pencil and a pen, which I do every day, and draw. If I could feel that natural with computers, then I could collaborate with somebody living anywhere in the world who speaks a different language and has a different culture. Intelligent machines can help us communicate and get into a natural creative flow. This is one of the promises of artificial intelligence.

Can you talk a little bit more about how machine learning is affecting creative tools?
The economy before was all about consistency. How can we make one thing to scale and do that one thing really well, which built amazing services like Uber. But now with machine learning, people can focus on expressing their uniqueness in how they draw or create content. We're seeing tools that are going to be able to provide far more ways of expressing yourself. And these individualized modes of making can only be enacted by understanding the data—by understanding you and providing services that fit your unique needs. Artificial intelligence has made this approach possible. I don't believe that you build technology and suddenly society changes around it, though. I actually think society demands something and there's a bit of a rush, then people find a way to build technology to meet that demand.

PATTIE MAES, PHD
Interview

Pattie Maes leads the MIT Media Lab's Fluid Interfaces research group, which thrives on radically reinventing the human-machine experience. With a background in artificial intelligence (AI) and human-computer interaction, she focuses on cognitive enhancement, or how immersive and wearable systems can assist people with memory, attention, learning, decision making, communication, and well-being.

What role will contextual data play in the future of interface design?

Today, our devices encourage a lot of task switching and multitasking, which has been shown to be ineffective for getting stuff done. It also provokes anxiety in people. I think tomorrow's devices will help us be more in the moment and more focused on the current task. They will, because of their context awareness, give us information that is relevant to what we're doing, as opposed to pulling us out of the current task with some information about something completely unrelated.

What are some of the challenges around creating these kinds of contextual interaction experiences?

My research group ask questions of privacy, control, and understanding. We ask if the person knows the limitations of the technology assisting them, which is also really important. For a GPS system or a self-driving car, for example, you will have to understand when that system will fail and what it can and cannot do, so you don't make assumptions that the system is going to do the right thing. Dependency is the fourth question: Do we want to rely completely on the system to perform a certain skill on our behalf? Are we okay with losing that ability ourselves? Or is it more important, for example, that the system trains the user and teaches the user how to do something? We have these conversations in my research group, but I feel like these things shouldn't necessarily just be up to us and that we should have larger discussions.

One project that we worked on was wellness oriented. It was a system that helps a person breathe more slowly and deeply when they're anxious. One approach that you could take is to build a system that influences your breathing in an unconscious way. People have built systems like this before. But, of course, if an interface unconsciously influences a person to breathe more slowly when they're anxious, then they're never going to learn and internalize the skill of calming themselves down. It's better to build a system that teaches them, "Look, if you feel anxious, try breathing. Try doing ten breaths in and out slowly." You can then visualize, for

"With a lot of data, you can make impressive systems and deliver functionality that may look intelligent to the naive outsider, but actually, it's a sophisticated pattern recognition type of approach."
—Pattie Maes

example, how doing this affects their heart rate or their electrodermal activity. People can then internalize the skill and understand it without relying on the machine. We have these discussions all the time.

What issues around AI are crucial for young designers to think about?

AI systems will increasingly be assisting us. There's a lot of talk in the press about AI systems replacing people. But I think that what will happen more frequently is that we'll have to work with AI systems that give us advice and recommendations in the moment, related to whatever problem we're dealing with. One issue that we are looking at is to what extent people believe or trust the AI system. We're looking at this whole issue of the effects of the system being able to explain itself. Does the person then trust the system more easily?

Also, are people too quick to trust these systems without asking for an explanation? That seems to be the case. They're not critical enough of the recommendations of the system. We noticed this already way back in the nineties, when we were developing recommendation systems for music and books. We noticed that if the system made a recommendation for music that the person may like based on their personal data, people too readily just agreed with

the recommendations. If the system would say, "You would like the Beatles a lot, they would say, yes, this system understands me amazingly well. I do like the Beatles a lot. Look how right it is." But in many cases, the data showed that this person previously had rated the Beatles as neutral, not something that they liked a lot. So we are looking at how we can encourage people to be skeptical about recommendations. We look at what kinds of explanations may help and how the system should frame its recommendations to encourage more skepticism.

There will be critical scenarios in which this is important, like a doctor who is getting support from some system that makes a diagnosis. They will have to not just too readily assume that the system is making the right decision. They will have to ask for explanations and supporting evidence. That whole issue is still unresolved. The whole issue of AI systems even being able to give an explanation is something being worked on right now. We also have to look at the design and the human side of things and at how to give explanations in a way that people, again, can be critical and careful about the recommendations they receive and whether they should react to them. This is very much a design question, more so than an AI-system question.

PATRICK HEBRON
Interview

A software developer, designer, teacher, and author, Patrick Hebron leads the Machine Intelligence Design team at Adobe. His work focuses on the emerging intersections between machine-learning, design tools, programming languages, and operating systems.

What kind of relationship will unfold between humans and machines?

The path forward is for us to celebrate difference. The world is full of human thinkers. If we want human thinking, we should probably go to humans for it. There are a lot of them. I don't see the sense in trying to replicate the human perceptual system. One of the interesting things about artificial intelligence is the prospect of having another intelligent species on this planet. This is of real value because it holds a mirror up to the nature of our intelligence and to intelligence in general. It also brings a new form of intelligence into the world, which can be constructed as a harmonious counterpart to our intelligence.

DeepMind's work on gameplaying has been particularly inspirational to me. In one of its games against the human champion, Lee Sedol, AlphaGo played a now-famous move that the commentators initially thought was a mistake. Ultimately, they realized that this was a brilliant move—a move that defied three thousand years of human strategic wisdom. It discovered this novel strategy through its own intuition rather than adhering to someone else's preconceived notions of how to play the game. There's a real value in that. After the match against Lee Sedol, DeepMind built a new version of its system that only learned from its own gameplay and had no contact whatsoever with any human-played games. This new version was substantially better than the previous. It's amazing what a fresh perspective can do!

Though Go is just a game, we can start to leverage this kind of strength in other things too. To be clear, this strength is not a matter of raw intellectual horsepower. It's more a matter of how we can commit the machine's intellect to a particular domain or task. We are temporally confined by our life spans but can build ideas across numerous lifespans by communicating with one another, by writing ideas down and sharing them. Machines also have limited life spans, of course. But they can approach communication somewhat differently than us. When humans communicate ideas to one another, they start from some sort of mental representation and distill it into concrete language, which is then interpreted by the listener back into a new mental representation. A lot can be lost in translation. A lot of the nuance can be lost to the low fidelity of language.

"How can we bridge the perceptual gap? Humans and machines are both perceptual entities. But their mode of perception is fairly different from one another, regardless of raw horsepower."—Patrick Hebron

With machines, we can set up thousands of learners to interact with a given task or material and discover a wide variety of unique approaches. Ultimately though, we can take each of those machines' mental representations and merge them together without having to pass through a low-fidelity language. So a thousand separate Go players don't need to result in a thousand separate Go players, they can result in one extremely intelligent one—a player that has benefited from the integration of many different strategic approaches. Of course, our approach to knowledge transfer also has its strengths. The loss of fidelity through language may be a good thing in some ways—a kind of one step backwards, two steps forward kind of progress that leads to a constant pruning and reorienting of human knowledge over the ages. In any case, having different sorts of intellectual strength in the world is a good thing. As we bring these technologies into our lives, we need to think about how we situate them in relation to what we each are good at.

When it comes to design, there are always going to be factors that will have to come from humans. Autodesk has done some interesting work on constraint satisfaction. In this framework, rather than designing the specifics of a bicycle, the human instead appoints particular attributes they would like the system to

include—for example, they want a bike to be both fast and lightweight. The machine then tries many different possibilities, running each through a physics simulation to determine which best expresses the desired combination of attributes. This kind of system can be quite successful in meeting its stated goals. But, of course, in bicycle design, there are many important considerations beyond performance characteristics. Is the design a good fit for the human physiology? Will a human know how to sit on it? If the bicycle is too different from anything that the user has encountered before, then the bike may not be very useful. Human-machine symbiosis means balancing the machine's ability to open up possibility spaces with the human designer's ability to mitigate that newness against historical legacy and issues of familiarity.

In my work at Adobe, the focus is somewhat different because objective optimization criteria, such as a bike's speed and weight, are generally less applicable in the domain of graphic design and image editing. In this context, the machine can also help to make the possibility space more accessible to and navigable by users. But it is clear from the start that a human must guide the process toward an outcome that will be deemed pleasing or useful by a human audience.

How will machine learning influence design practice in the future?

People have the initial reaction of, "Is this going to replace designers?" In some respects and to some extent, the answer is likely to be yes. Any massive paradigm shift is going to have uncomfortable growing pains. There's no denying that. But from another angle, this paradigm shift is not unique in its disruption to the organization and economies of how work is performed. For example, in architecture, the Florence Cathedral took about one hundred and forty years to go from initial conception to project completion. A much more complicated and recent building, the Burj Khalifa, took about five years. One of the key differences between those two projects is the advent of computer-aided design, or CAD, tools. These tools make it possible to conceive of systems that are too grand and complex for any one individual to keep all of their big picture goals and specific details in mind simultaneously. The importance of being able to scaffold complexity cannot be understated. If you look at the early versions of Adobe's Photoshop, many of the features are direct translations of concepts that existed in predigital tools—pens, scissors, and the like. Initially, designers approached these tools with the same tasks and the same aesthetic goals as they had before. Quickly, though, they started to see opportunities that were not possible from the capacities of a darkroom. They began to have ideas that would have required so many steps or such precision that those ideas would simply have not come to mind in the earlier context of paper and photographic emulsion. With digital tools, it became easier to scaffold certain types of processes and therefore to scaffold increasingly complex aesthetic goals. We are now entering another dramatic leap forward in this respect. Machine intelligence will enable creatives to do even more and to think even bigger.

Machine intelligence will also enable people to interact with design in a way that requires a lot less tool learning. Rather than you having to speak the language of the tool, you will be able to express your ideas in the form that you hold them. If you want to make the sky brighter, for example, rather than saying, "I need to select all of the pixels that represent sky and then go to this menu and drop down and go to the brightness slider," we can instead issue a semantically formulated command to simply make the sky brighter. That opens the door to more people; it democratizes the design process and leads to a greater volume of design work being created by a wider range of people. From an accessibility point of view, we can start to think about the machine understanding lots of different modes of input. Different people think in different ways—speech may be preferable for one person while demonstrative gestures may be preferable for another. There is a very real path to opening up new opportunities for human designers through these technologies. I am very excited about that and glad to be a part of it.

STEPHANIE YEE AND TONY CHU
Interview

Stephanie Yee is a data scientist in San Francisco. She enjoys thinking about data products and decision making under uncertainty. An economist at heart, she studied statistics because it helps the world make sense.

Tony Chu is a designer from Vancouver, Canada. He works in interaction design for technical systems, with a focus on machine-learning and data visualization.

Why should designers care about machine learning?

TC: I often tell designers: abundant, cheap predictions are going to change the material that you're designing with, and you better get used to understanding how to work with it.

Do you find that designers are now coming to you machine learning literate?

TC: They're still getting their feet wet. People used to come to me and say, "What is this? Why should I care?" They're now coming to me and saying, "I know I should care, but how do I learn more?"

What do you wish designers could get through their heads before they come to a data scientist to talk about a project?

SY: I wish designers understood that the tool kit is actually much larger than they realize. Data scientists know what's possible within this space. And the constraints, people's intuition about what might be hard or easy, take time to build.

TC: I'd want designers to come to data scientists with a bigger framing of the problem, so they can solve it together. If designers go to the data scientist and say, "Hey, here is the user need, and here are the kind of jobs to be done. Here is the experience that we want the user to have." Then your data-science partners can be your thought partners instead of just a deliverer of an algorithm.

Can you speak to this statement from one of Tony's lectures: "Machine learning is never perfect, nor does it need to be."

SY: You're never going to have a perfect prediction. By the time something becomes a data-science problem or a machine-learning problem, there's uncertainty that's inherent. That's why you need these methods. The expectation that it's not perfect is helpful because that's part of the definition of the problem.

TC: I focus on if it's not perfect, what do you do? If you're designing the experience assuming that it's perfect, you're going to be unhappy with the results. Designers are taught to not just design for the happy path. My ask of designers is to think about it as another kind of failure case. You have to work with data scientists to understand what are likely failure cases and what you should do about them. Then be aware that you have to design for those. That's a part of your practice now as a designer.

What excites you as you look to the future of the technology?

SY: People are going to improve lots of different decisions because we can take an advanced machine-learning-oriented approach. What excites me is there are certain disciplines or places where ML is just starting to get a hold, where the impact on people's lives can be quite substantial.

One place is the last-mile human element that you need to have in the healthcare setting. Machine learning can help guide people's attention via a prediction or help us figure out how to manage our time. Time is a finite, precious resource. A lot of useful ML methods and techniques are not the most advanced. You don't necessarily need computer vision to solve, for example, how to make a case manager most efficient or how to help a case manager best be able to serve patients.

TC: Since I'm not dug into the day-to-day development of these tools, I think about how they get applied. Over the next ten years, I expect these tools will become more pliable to designers. I already see designers and artists who say, "OK, let's take a GAN model or something like GPT-3 and muck around with it and shape it to do weird things." We are getting to a point where you no longer need to learn PyTorch and figure out what gradient descent is and do all that stuff to get a machine-learning model going. It's just going to get easier. It's getting democratized.

Designers will find ways to apply machine learning in places where they may not yet have obvious economic value. They will say, "Let's just throw it against the wall and see what sticks." To me that is exciting from a tooling perspective, since that's what I work on at Facebook. In ten years, designers and other folks should be able to say, "Hey, I gathered a bunch of data. Under these circumstances, I want it to do this thing" and then the machine learning model should be able to figure out how to make that connection happen.

Then designers can go figure out what it is that enables. It's hard to speculate what would be possible. But the idea of being able to shape and ship a machine-learning model based on just mucking around with a bunch of training data. That's an exciting place.

What else is important for designers to know about machine learning?

TC: I know you intentionally skipped ethics and bias in this discussion, but I think it is very important. The other thing of importance, especially for designers, is that there are specific things that machine learning and data science are good at today. And there are other things that they are just not capable of doing in the foreseeable future. Designers need to understand the difference and be able to tell if somebody is a snake oil salesman. You can do a lot of things that are productive with basic machine-learning tools today, like being able to do associative learning at scale. That is what machine-learning models are built to do—they figure out relationships.

But, for example, there are no good machine-learning systems for dealing with causality and understanding. That kind of reasoning is not automatic. If you are a designer and you don't understand that, then you're going to either not be able to take full advantage of what it's capable of doing or you're going to make bad promises to people.

The most clear example of this for me recently is GPT-3. It looks like it's having a conversation with you, but it's just finding the answer found on the internet that seemed most relevant. That's not the same thing at all. If you understand that that's the game that's being played, then great, you know how to design for the field. If somebody asks you a question that there's no relevant answer to, it should fall back to a human. That's an experience you can design. Whereas if you think this machine understands what it's saying and you expect it to say something intelligent back, you're going to be disappointed.

SY: My thoughts go back to the question that you asked before: what do I wish designers knew before talking to a data scientist? With any machine-learning system either the quality or the quantity of the data really matters. For a machine-learning model there are two inputs. There's the data available that you use to train it and then there's the expert tuning and tinkering. If you don't have either high-quality or enough data, then your model is not going to be helpful.

The models that tend to be in widest use are usually not the most complex. And often, you want as simple a model as possible. People often say, "We have this great proprietary machine-learning model." But what really matters is the data itself. The model is more of a by-product to get there. There's an extensive user manual that goes with it.

But if you're looking at it as a designer, it's like, "OK, is there going to be rich data? And can the experience that I'm designing generate more data?" Framing machine learning in that context, especially for designers, is novel. But it's something that is valuable. If I'm a data scientist— and there's something that generates a lot of data and also is machine-learning oriented—that's heaven.

TC: I tell the designers on my team that the data has to come from somewhere. And often, the data comes from the interactions that you design. There's two sides of it: If you design the interaction poorly, you're going to capture bad data. And that's not going to help anyone. But if you design a novel interaction that suddenly captures a new type of data, then that's great. And that's where a lot of value can come from. A lot of interesting work is going to come out of social networks and video games and things like that where you're asking people to interact. By capturing that data, you can learn new things and maybe take on some of those big questions that Stephanie brought up before when she talked about the last mile.

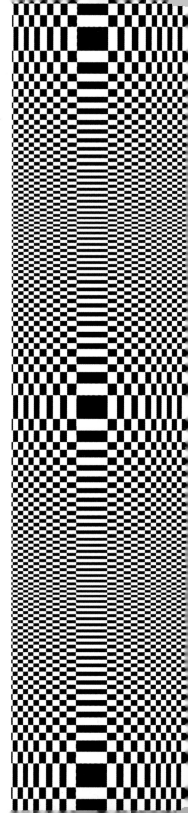

Thinking Design + Conversation
Paul Pangaro

As a human-computer interaction professor of practice at
Carnegie Mellon University, Paul Pangaro works at the intersection of design, humanities, and theory to generate richer
human interactions, with technology and without. His research
centers on how conversation can be facilitated—between and
among humans, machines, organizations, and individuals.

When I think of design, I immediately think of conversation.
Why?

When I say *design* I mean the deliberate, thoughtful,
caring, explicit act of doing something that takes an existing
situation and brings about a preferred one. You might hear
Herbert Simon in this definition of design, but I hear what
came before Simon, which is cybernetics, the art and science
of systems that have purpose. Designers are purposeful—we
hope. They decide on improvements or preferences, which,
in turn, come from their values. When we—as designers or
just human beings—observe our own observing, we see that
we are *choosing* what we pay attention to (or ignore). So we
become aware of our subjectivity. This begins a conversation
with ourselves. Once we look at our own looking, we realize
that we are constantly bringing our *own purpose and values*
into our act of observing. We become aware of our personal
biases. *We realize we are responsible for our values.* Notice:
when we see our subjectivity and biases, we are responsible
for being transparent about them. Now we are thinking of
ethical design.

Design in the twenty-first century has moved beyond
objects and products and into services and platforms:
Google, Amazon, and Facebook are the most ubiquitous and
consuming. The resulting complex mesh of interfaces and
devices, hardware and software, networks and databases

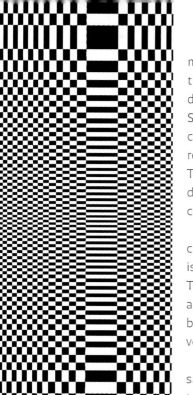

must operate seamlessly without requiring attention from the user. Given the inherent complexity of these systems, design today is beyond the capacity of an individual designer. So not only do we designers need a pragmatic grasp of the complexity of systems but also that creating these systems requires collaboration, and collaboration means conversation. This is why I construe design as conversation. And as designers we are responsible for bringing proficiency in collaboration and conversation into our design practice.

But wait, there's more to thinking about design and conversation. I believe that as designers the best we can do is create conditions in which *others can have conversations*. Through conversation, others can clarify *their* values, uncover and define *what they want* for themselves, and ultimately become *who they want to become*. Enabling others to converse is "design for conversation."

Now I have to acknowledge that bringing up "conversation" in the context of today's technology usually means talking to a machine and having it talk back. We can get excited when we ask a conversational agent a question by voice and get an answer. *I say that's pretty boring*. I can do that with a search engine by typing and clicking. (Hands-free with a voice interface is great but that difference alone is not enough.) I want a conversational interface in which I can fluidly explore possibilities in threaded exchanges that are explorations and speculations and thereby open new spaces for myself and others. In other words: Can I just have a real conversation, please?

I don't find that today's voice interfaces help foster real conversation. They're not bad at coordination and simple transactions: "What's the weather?" "Turn on the light!" "How many people live in Pittsburgh?" These types of interactions are good for buying dish soap, which is the origin of the most conversational agents anyway—they are agents of commerce. They are not designed to foster collaboration, to learn, to agree, to decide on coordinated action to achieve our shared goals. Why not?

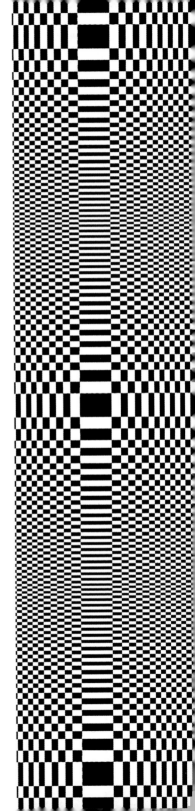

Beyond productive verbal exchanges, what interactions are rich enough to be called real conversations? Sometimes: writing to one another, whether in chat windows or email or documents. (Researchers write papers that create conversational interchange across schools of thought.) I also mean the dialogue we construct in our own heads as we read, learn, reconcile new information, agree, or disagree. When I say conversation, please don't think of speech alone but think of a dialectic in which you learn something important, perhaps change your mind or your desires, and maybe even become someone different.

Today's technology for speaking with machines, wondrous as it is, is still a far cry from enabling the kind of natural conversation we have with ourselves and others. I want to change that. For example, I want to build interfaces that create "conversation with content," even when the content is text and the user is reading and maybe rolling a mouse or finger over a window in a browser.

Conversation comprises "turns"—after all, to converse means "turning together." How do we get a machine to respond meaningfully in its turn?

I've built software that fosters conversation in a cybernetic sense—regulating the interaction toward the participants' purpose, such as to learn, to collaborate, to act. One valuable approach is to moderate how much "newness" is offered to the user. If a conversational response is not novel in some way, it's repetitive and likely boring. At the other extreme, if it's too novel and "out there," then it's hard to grasp and you may have little idea of its meaning. Of course the question is, how does a machine measure what is novel? Let's say the software knows where you are in the content (say, a paragraph on a page); what you have seen before (since you've been "in conversation" for a while and across sessions); and how you have reacted to it (like it, don't get it, more/less of this). Then the software can build an approximate but useful model of your knowledge. So if you say/type something to the machine, it could decide its

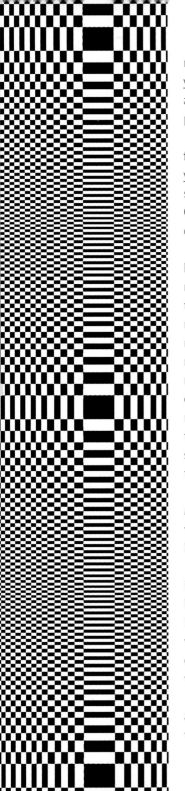

response by choosing something *highly related* to where you are but also new to you. (Think of that colleague who always takes your conversations to interesting and unexpected places.)

What makes such a conversation interesting? Are you feeling connected to new ideas that respect the ideas that you just spoke about? Are you engaged, maybe even unconsciously, in creating a new and interesting world of ideas? Can we write algorithms to do that in an interface that offers content in the manner of human-to-human conversation?

We can, and I've done it, but I was only reworking heuristics written decades before and embodied in electro-mechanical systems, before digital was available. One of these systems responded with a light show based on a musician's improvisation. Another was life-sized, robotic mobiles that mostly "talked among themselves" but also responded to humans who came into their loop. Some were more explicitly learning machines, that is, adaptive educational environments that tracked what the user knew, responded to specific curiosity, and presented novel material that engaged and provoked. These machines enabled conversations—yet none of these machines ever spoke or listened to anyone talking.

I'm describing the work of cybernetician Gordon Pask, a *maker* before the term existed, who, from the 1950s to the 1970s, built interactive capabilities unlike any that the world has seen, before or since.

It's much easier to build Paskian machines today. But instead, the big platform companies use complex coding to build machine-learning systems based on Big Data, aggregating thousands and millions of other people's behaviors. So when I get a recommendation from Amazon for what to buy, or from Google for what to read (or, increasingly, what to buy whose recommendation is it? *Whose* purpose does it serve?

Let's say you ask me, "Where is the best pizza nearby?" and I respond, "Right across the street at Luigi's Pizza!" But what if you then asked me, "Why is it the best pizza?" and I responded, "Screw you, I'm not going to tell you!" Would you talk to me again? Would you trust my advice? But wait... I just described Google! Why do we accept behavior from *a machine* that we would never accept from a *person*?

Artificial intelligence determines more and more of the world we see and the world we live in. It chooses for us; decides what we should buy or read or even think. Notice: it makes these decisions based on *who we were* (even if just minutes ago) rather than *who we are this moment*. Search engine results and recommendations for what to buy or watch are about the past. So when a machine uses my prior responses and doesn't connect and resonate with *who I am right now*, I might as well be *dead*. Questions, in contrast, are alive—questions are "of the now." Why can't our machines present us with questions, if we want them, rather than answers based on who we used to be? Who might I be right at this instant? What choice would I make *right now*?

I fear that without some retreat from Big Data and a renewal of *the importance of the individual in the here-and-now*, we will sink further along a path of no return from the mechanization of who we are as human beings. The parable of Luigi's Pizza spotlights the designer's responsibility to build systems that interact honestly and transparently and in real-time—to create conditions for open-ended conversations. For me, anything less is unethical.

Most of us want the world to evolve and new technology to bring about change. But instead of beginning with what we wish to change, can we ask, what do we wish to *conserve*? What do we humans want to keep? What are our *values*?

When we define what we wish to conserve, we open a space of possibilities in which change can occur. Then we are free to explore what we want to be new—and lessen the risk of losing who we are and what we cherish as human beings.

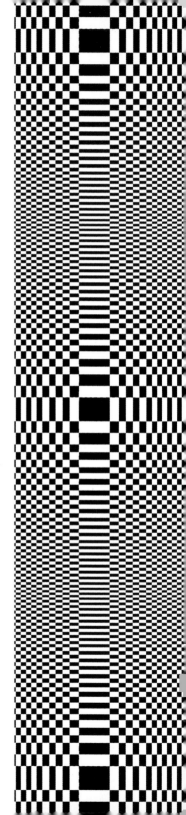

FIG 29. MUSICOLOUR. In 1953, Gordon Pask built a series of machines that engaged a musician in an open-ended "conversation" by projecting lights in response to the music—but then becoming "bored" (nonresponsive) so that the musician would modify their playing to maintain engagement.

FIG 30. COLLOQUY OF MOBILES REPLICA AT CENTRE POMPIDOU. In 1968, Pask continued to explore conversational machines with his human-sized interacting robotic mobiles engaged in a courtship dance of cooperation and competition through light and sound. In 2020, Paul Pangaro and T.J. McLeish displayed their full-scale working replica in Paris.

More than Human-Centered Design

Anab Jain

Anab Jain is founder and director of Superflux, a future-facing studio that takes on the challenges of the new millennium through thoughtful, provocative design. A professor at the University of Applied Arts in Vienna, she is also bringing to students her vision as a designer, futurist, and filmmaker.

Perhaps the best, or maybe worst, place to start is by exposing my greatest fear. I am scared of death. But not as scared as I used to be. From around the age of ten and into my early teens, I collected, in the archive of my head, hundreds of my imagined deaths. Traveling in the train through the dark Indian desert, I would imagine being shot from somewhere far in the distance. Or rushing through chaotic Ahmedabad traffic, I would imagine the railway bridge falling on me. Even though it would have been easy enough, I resisted the lure of religious spirituality—and instead found my spiritual home in cinema. It is from this that I look to the future, a future that, when my son is my age, will be incredibly worrying.

Based on the current global projections for both the massive increase in human population and the huge decrease in available land to feed them from, our team at Superflux worked on a project exploring a future where the Western world has moved from abundance to scarcity. We imagined living in a future city with repeated flooding, periods with almost no food in supermarkets, economic instabilities, broken supply chains. We asked ourselves, what can we do to not just survive, but prosper in such a world? What food can we eat? This inquiry became the basis of our installation *Mitigation of Shock*, commissioned by the Centre for Contemporary Culture Barcelona and curated by José Luis de Vincente.

"How do we imagine different worlds within the current political landscape?"—Anab Jain

The installation transports you to a London flat, perhaps in the year 2050 or so—when my son might be around my age. At first glance, you're in a seemingly comfortable living space designed for a world of automated living, global trade, and material abundance. Then on closer inspection, you realize the apartment has been adapted to a future it was never meant to inhabit. Discarded newspapers and a radio show reflect the tensions of this new world; recipes in the kitchen reveal the change in food production, storage, and consumption. Experimental food production occupies space once given to relaxation—transforming the apartment into a space for growing and producing food. Towering silver stacks of mushrooms, cabbages, and chili plants flourish in an optimally lit indoor environment.

As part of the installation, Jon Ardern, co-founder of Superflux, built a food computer from scratch—something he hadn't done before. We used the soil-free, nutrient-enriched water vapor technique of fogponics to grow things quickly. We wanted to build them in the cheapest way possible: from salvaged, abandoned, and repurposed materials. Turning today's waste into tomorrow's dinner.

One of the things that I found incredibly fascinating was the growth of the humble mushroom—this mycelium we tried to grow in so many ways. We used Arduinos and ultrasonic fog to control the humidity in the DIY polythene-clad box that had become our fruiting chamber. For a while nothing much happened. Then suddenly it began to find its right environment, or rather, our human activities and disturbances, both planned and unplanned, had created the optimum conditions for it to grow. Eventually, it grew into this beautiful brightly colored and quite delicious form. This direct experience drew us into the world of many interacting species. It provided a useful vantage point for knowing ourselves as participants in more complex human and nonhuman relationships.

This inspired me to think of a bigger picture, and instead of the established "user-centered design" narrative so loved by technology companies and design schools alike, I considered a "more-than-human" centered approach where human beings are not at the center of the universe and the center of everything. Where we consider ourselves as deeply entangled in relationships with other species and nonhuman entities.

Our profession, and those we have served, after a long time, finally has come around to the idea of human-centered design, which is important for many reasons, especially when designing for diverse users and communities. But, in a broader context, as multispecies anthropologist Anne Galloway writes: "What if we deny that human beings are exceptional? What if we stop speaking and listening only to ourselves?"

Galloway continues, "Complementary ways of thinking, doing, and making emphasize the practice of care and imagination and challenge us to work with, not against, vulnerability, humility and interdependence." Interdependence is a powerful concept for me: different participants—human and nonhuman—are emotionally, economically, ecologically, or morally interdependent on each other. And this reliance is acknowledged. I think this perspective is something that would be very meaningful for many of us to consider—whether we're interaction, service, or UX designers, entrepreneurs, researchers, or people who put things out in the world for others "to use."

Apart from climate change, another reason to consider this form of interdependence is much closer to home. Today, we are already living amid other kinds of nonhuman entities, increasingly autonomous things and systems that are very

"Modernism was essentially an unquestioning pursuit of a 'better future'—and that is perhaps the reason we are in this situation."—Anab Jain

"If you can move beyond quick fixes, we become open to the strange and the unknown, the ambiguous and the uncertain, the weird and the provisional."
—Anab Jain

seductive. But beneath the gloss of technological utopia, it is becoming obvious how these computers, tools, and machines that we have created in order to master the world are remastering us: our politics, the way we relate to each other, and the world around us.

We don't exist in isolation. We never have. Now we are entering a time when we can no longer live in the illusion of isolation; we can either embrace this new understanding and work with its implications or face the hubris of our inaction. I want to conclude with a call to arms, a call to closely consider our relationships (both human and nonhuman) with the world in which we live and work. A call to consider ourselves in relationship with, not as masters of, the deeper ecology around and within us. And to embody this in our actions. I will leave you with this quote by the sixteenth-century philosopher Miyamoto Musashi: "Think lightly of yourself and deeply of the world."

FIG 31. *MITIGATION OF SHOCK* **(LONDON).** This immersive installation for the Centre for Contemporary Culture Barcelona (CCCB), created by designers at Superflux, makes environmental impact tangible. Set in a future apartment, the domestic space includes adaptive tools for surviving the rigors of climate change and food insecurity, i.e., experimental food production stacks. The installation projects current climate-change data into the future, asking visitors to experience how we might learn to adapt.

FIG 32. *MITIGATION OF SHOCK* **(SINGAPORE).** Designers at Superflux created this installation for *2219: Futures Imagined*, an exhibition at ArtScience Museum in celebration of the Singapore Bicentennial. The installation allows participants to experience a speculative Singapore in which residents have adapted in radical ways to a future life of extreme weather, economic uncertainty, and disrupted supply chains. The resulting tools of survival are less tech-centric than *Mitigation of Shock* (London), looking, instead, to a nonanthropocentric way of life that recognizes our place within a complex ecology. Both of the *Mitigation of Shock* installations surface human interdependence with many kinds of nonhuman entities—both biological and inorganic.

CHAPTER THREE

Predict the Way

Machine learning (ML)—for all the good—can be dangerous like nothing else designers have faced before. As Joanna Peña-Bickley, head of research and design at Alexa Devices at Amazon, notes, "We need to fear the consequences of our work more than we have in the past."[1] Designers cannot blindly apply this technology without the risk of subjecting humans to discrimination, surveillance, and/or manipulation, not just individually but at scale. ML's facade of objectivity hides a plethora of moments in which humans reach in to tweak predictive systems.[2] And, with each tweak, social and political factors shape the ultimate output, more often than not to the detriment of the most vulnerable.

As noted by researcher Kate Crawford of the AI Now Institute, "Understanding the politics within AI systems matters more than ever, as they are quickly moving into the architecture of social institutions: deciding whom to interview for a job, which students are paying attention in class, which suspects to arrest, and much else."[3] ML reaches into citizens' lives, opening, as well as obstructing, opportunities. These invisible systems are creeping into public and private spaces—even the most intimate parts of our bodies and minds.

WHAT GETS LEFT OUT?

To understand the politics of ML, let's start with the act of classification. Supervised and unsupervised learning models place incoming data into buckets—more precisely, classes or clusters. For supervised learning, experts determine specific classes early in the process and then label training data accordingly. Unsupervised learning also divides data into buckets. In unsupervised learning, however, the model, rather than humans, analyzes the structure of the data, delineates the pattern recognition outputs, and then labels the training data. As in supervised learning, this training data becomes the "ground truth," the basis for future predictions. Let's look a bit harder at this concept of training data and the process around it.

Envision squeezing the chaotic, messy, abstract nature of life into discrete labeled buckets. What can be contained and what invariably must be left out? What happens to sexuality, race, gender, emotions, relationships, and so on, that fall in between? Various researchers have pointed out the limitations and political implications of knowledge produced via a classification process.[4] In their project Excavating AI, researchers Kate Crawford and Trevor Paglen look at this problem specifically in relation to image recognition technology. They ask: "What sorts of politics are at work when pictures are paired with labels, and what are the implications when they are used to train technical systems?"[5]

Their research examines ImageNet, a highly influential dataset of over fourteen million labeled images. Computer-vision researchers worldwide have frequently used this convenient, accessible image database since its origination in 2009.[6] Far from challenging stereotypical assumptions, as Crawford and Paglen demonstrate, datasets like ImageNet reflect back existing societal bias. Crawford and Paglen look at specific categories and associated images included by the system. Their work probes the implications of treating social, relational categories, such as "person," in the same way as "something naturalized or fixed, like labeling a cat or a chair." Artificial intelligence (AI) systems, Crawford asserts, "are rarifying fluid categories and then making claims with absolute certainty."[7]

For example, Crawford and Paglen's research found 2,833 subcategories in ImageNet under the top-level category "Person." Upon examination, troubling terms emerge from these subcategories. Racist and misogynistic slurs appear, such as "Bad Person, Call Girl, Drug Addict, Closet Queen, Convict, Crazy, Failure, Flop, Fucker, Hypocrite, Jezebel, Kleptomaniac, Loser…Spinster, Streetwalker, Stud, Tosser, Unskilled Person, Wanton, Waverer, and Wimp." The images classified under each of these subcategories are telling.[8] Through such categories, the worldview behind the dataset takes form. Unquestioned gendered, racialized, ableist, and ageist assumptions abound. According to ImageNet, who is or is not "wanton"? Who is or is not a "bad person"? Who is or is not a "fucker"?

Crawford and Paglen warn: "To impose order onto an undifferentiated mass, to ascribe phenomena to a category—that is, to name a thing—is in turn a means of reifying the existence of that category." Datasets like ImageNet reinforce societal bias rather than calling it into question. The effects of this reverberate throughout industry and academia as other researchers blindly propagate this same bias when they adopt such datasets to conveniently train their own algorithms. Crawford and Paglen urge individuals to examine the architecture and contents of all AI training sets, to peer deeply into the black box, "because they are already used to examine us."[9]

BLACK BOX: a metaphor in ML that refers to a human's inability to see the internal workings of a system

"What does fairness look like when computers shape decision making? Who is creating the future, and how can we ensure that these creators reflect diverse communities and complex social dynamics?"
—Mimi Onuoha and Mother Cyborg

But are designers responsible for the contents of training sets? Does this lie beyond our purview? When designers create interfaces or digital products that utilize machine learning, they put training data into action. A few years ago, my students worked with a company to explore the privacy issues around embedding image recognition in retail spaces. We considered privacy from a variety of perspectives, prototyping many possibilities for increasing user control of data, but asked no questions around the image dataset being used. We never considered possible discrimination that could result from tech that might misidentify or even fail to register certain populations—the very populations that we were, ironically, attempting to serve. If designers don't educate themselves around these issues, we will unknowingly marginalize and even oppress populations.

Quite a bit of useful research has been done specifically around bias and AI training sets. In the Gender Shades project, Joy Buolamwini and Timnit Gebru analyzed two commonly used facial recognition datasets, IJB-A and Adience. They found that these datasets were "overwhelmingly composed of lighter-skinned subjects (79.6% for IJB-A and 86.2% for Adience)." They then introduced a more phenotypically balanced face dataset and used it to evaluate three commercial gender classification systems by skin type and by intersectional subgroups that combined gender and skin type. Their findings: "darker-skinned females are the most misclassified group (with error rates of up to 34.7%)," and "all [image] classifiers performed best for lighter individuals and males overall."[10] [Fig. 34] An ML system is only as inclusive as the training data fed into it; in this case, primarily lighter-skinned males.

PHENOTYPICAL: the observable physical or biochemical characteristics of a biological entity

INTERSECTIONAL: a theoretical framework that explores how multiple facets of an individual's social and political identities come together to result in systems of discrimination

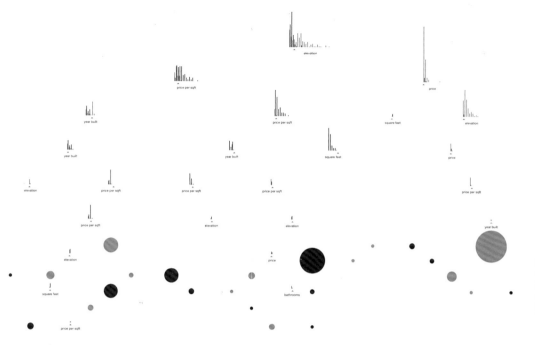

FIG 33. A VISUAL INTRODUCTION TO MACHINE LEARNING.
Stephanie Yee and Tony Chu, the founders of R2D3,
use interactive design to express statistical thinking.
The resulting visualizations explain machine learning
to novices through storytelling and interaction. The
segment included above demonstrates to users how data
might flow through a decision tree as a model is trained.

Gender Classifier	Female Subjects Accuracy	Male Subjects Accuracy	Error Rate Diff.
Microsoft	89.3%	97.4%	8.1%
FACE**	78.7%	99.3%	20.6%
IBM	79.7%	94.4%	14.7%

FIG 34. GENDER SHADES. In this study of
gender classification via facial analysis,
researchers Joy Buolamwini and Timnit Gebru
found that all the companies included in the
study performed better on lighter-skinned
subjects than darker-skinned subjects.

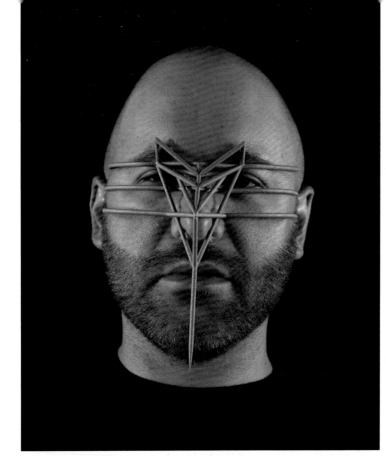

FIG 35. FACE CAGES. According to creator Zach Blas, "Face Cages is a dramatization of the abstract violence of the biometric diagram." Blas, in collaboration with three other queer artists— micha cárdenas, Elle Mehrmand, Paul Mpagi Sepuya—makes and then wears the masks in endurance performances for video. The performances emphasize biometrics as harmful reductions by emphasizing "the irreconcilability of the biometric diagram with the materiality of the human face itself—and the violence that occurs when the two are forced to coincide."[11]

Counterclockwise from Top:
Zach Blas Endurance Performances, Face Cage 1: Zach Blas, 2015; Face Cage 2: with Elle Mehrmand, 2014; Face Cage 3: with micha cárdenas, 2014; Face Cage 4: with Paul Mpagi Sepuya, 2016.

As noted by these researchers, such findings are particularly worrisome in relation to healthcare and law enforcement. We can easily envision, for example, decreased diagnostic accuracy for people of color by automated skin cancer detection systems or misidentification of faces by the algorithmic computer vision systems adopted by law enforcement.[12] In fact, Buolamwini and Gebru's warning of possible misidentification of suspects by facial recognition systems came eerily true in 2020 when an innocent Black man was wrongfully arrested in Michigan based on an inaccurate facial recognition match.[13] American society has since begun to flag the dangers of facial recognition in public spheres, particularly around law enforcement, both for its documented discriminatory inaccuracy and for the ease with which this tech can surveil and harass individuals. In Hong Kong, for example, police used facial recognition to track down protesters weeks after demonstrations, while, simultaneously, protesters used facial recognition to identify and dox plainclothes cops.[14] Companies like IBM, Amazon, and Microsoft have put their research temporarily on pause, while some communities have instituted bans in public spaces.[15] In the face of market pressures to continue developing the technology, the future of facial recognition in the US remains unresolved.

In addition to the problematic bias currently found in much image recognition technology, particularly around training data, ML technology can marginalize individuals in other ways. The process of gathering data via sensors can erase or confuse the detection and identification of certain individuals. In chapter one, we discussed the potential for ML capabilities to meet the needs of unique users, such as individuals with disabilities. And there is tremendous potential for systems to track and respond to these needs. However, the optimization—and the fairness—of ML systems depends in large part on the gathering of accurate data for training, as we discussed earlier. Increasingly, biometric sensors gather data about human behavior.[16] Shoshana Amielle Magnet, in her

DOX: to maliciously publish an individual's private information on the internet book *When Biometrics Fail*, questions who "exactly biometric systems can reliably identify." She points out that "biometric scanners are consistently reported to have difficulty scanning the hands of Asian women," while "iris scanners exclude wheelchair users and those with visual impairments." Skin diseases and scars, eye conditions like cataracts, and atypical speech can all lead to "unbiometrifiable" bodies—bodies effectively invisible to these sensors.[17] ML technology reflects how deeply discriminatory our society truly is, particularly around issues of disability.[18] Each time we work with machine learning, we have to raise the question of who is being left out by the data collection method.

Designers can also dig into the fairness of datasets by helping others examine the architecture and contents. Visualizations provide one clear path forward. Designers can visualize datasets, giving form to patterns in the data, enabling a range of people to quickly assess the problems and opportunities each dataset brings. Fernanda Viégas and Martin Wattenberg, cofounders of the People+AI Research (PAIR) Google initiative, created a tool called Facets Dive for inspecting each data point in a set of training data. In essence, the visualization encourages users to play with the data, examining it from different perspectives to better understand the content. PAIR has generated a range of additional tools as well, including the Embedding Projector which visually portrays the high dimensionality of a model as geometry, and TensorFlow.js, an ML library in the design friendly programming language Javascript.[19]

Designers can also use visualization to introduce the necessary statistical trade-offs around bias in a prediction. Data scientist Stephanie Yee and designer Tony Chu teamed up to create *A Visual Introduction to Machine Learning*, an interactive experience that mixes animation, visualization, and storytelling to quickly introduce ML to novices. [Fig 33] Part two of *A Visual Introduction* focuses on "Model Tuning and the Bias-Variance Tradeoff," enabling users to

BIOMETRICS: measurement and analysis of physical or behavioral human characteristics

HIGH DIMENSIONALITY: an extremely large number of dimensions

"What standards of 'normal' and 'ability' are produced and enforced by specific AI systems, and what are the costs of being understood as an 'outlier'?"
—Meredith Whittaker et al., AI Now Institute, NYU

experiment with statistical bias without a deep understanding of mathematics. Such tools translate datasets and models into accessible, tangible forms so that a range of researchers and stakeholders—social scientists, designers, product managers, developers, data scientists—can, together, explore the fairness of algorithmic systems.[20]

It's important to note, however, that all the visualizations and fairness tools in the world will not adequately address algorithmic bias if a diverse group is not involved throughout the development and deployment of AI projects. A 2018 report from the World Economic Forum asserts that "only 22% of AI professionals globally are women."[21] The AI Now Institute reported the following in 2019: "For black workers, the picture is even worse. For example, only 2.5% of Google's workforce is black, while Facebook and Microsoft are each at 4%."[22] The field of design is no better.[23] Time and again research has shown that the more diverse the team around the table, the more issues of bias will rise to the surface.[24] Serious efforts must be undertaken to take on "artificial intelligence's white guy problem," if we truly want to create fairer, more equitable AI.[25]

TALK BACK TO THE TECHNOLOGY
What other ML ethics issues should designers address? Within the current landscape, end users frequently don't understand how automated decisions—decisions that impact them directly—are made. Why is Facebook prioritizing some posts while hiding others? Why is Google serving up specific suggestions to me but not to my sister? Why is an autonomous vehicle turning left instead of right? Why did I not get that insurance rate, that loan, that job? Individuals struggle to trust black box decisions that refuse to explain why.

From a human-centered perspective, individuals need to be able to interrogate automated decisions at any point in an interaction to better understand the decision process and the limitations of the technology. Sarah Gold's studio, IF, worked with the drone insurance company Flock to create tools to do just this. (Drones, it seems, are pricey. They crash just like cars and airplanes.) Gold explains it this way:

> Flock developed an interface that helped commercial drone operators understand how the risk or the policy changed depending on [location] by providing a career risk score over the top of an interactive map....We then worked with Flock and the London School of Economics to look at that even further by looking at counterfactual explanations. I would describe this as almost an "if this then that," which is that if it is windy, the policy will be more expensive because the crash risk is higher. However, if the wind is low, the quote is cheaper. This kind of evidencing through real time data about how a particular automated decision is being made gives operators the ability to play with the boundaries of the decision making process....It was really encouraging to see a team uncovering how a technical system is working—not letting people believe it's magic.[26] [Fig. 36]

If a user doesn't understand how a decision is made, they have no way of holding the system accountable for bad decisions and no way of stepping in to improve outcomes. Without such information, they become the victims of these predictions.

Once end users understand the logic behind how specific algorithmic systems are making decisions, they can, when appropriate, add or remove data points to affect outcomes. Design researcher Caroline Sinders uses Spotify as an example of this in action. Why, she asks, should her Discover Weekly playlist be plagued by breakup songs long after the breakup has passed? Why can't she go in and adjust the data points herself to change the recommended songs?[27]

confirm your policy

51.5102, -0.1178
500m geofence

begins 16:02, 16 June 2020
ends 18:02, 16 June 2020

decision id 09C548E

Factors that influenced your quote:

Wind speed **35 km/h SE**
If below **20 km/h**, your quote
would have been cheaper

Chance of rain **88%**
If below **64%**, your quote
would have been cheaper

confirm your quote

FIG 36. FLOCK. This commercial-drone insurance company worked with Sarah Gold's studio, IF, to create an interface that might help their clients understand how automated decisions were being made around insurance rates. The interface surfaces factors, such as location, rainfall, wind speed, visibility, and temperature, which feed an automated risk score that determines cost.

FIG 37. AI CHEATSHEET. Alex Fefegha, founder of the design studio Comuzi, collaborated with colleagues Akil Benjamin and Sekyeong Kwon to demystify AI concepts through this straightforward tool for defining key AI terms. Much of Comuzi's work focuses on using design to start conversations with communities. Through such interactions, Fefegha wants to give people the knowledge needed to set their own AI boundaries.

F'xa

Your feminist guide
to AI bias

FIG 38. F'XA. Dr. Charlotte Webb and Conor Rigby, cofounders of the Feminist Internet collective, worked with design studio Comuzi to create this chatbot guide to AI bias. Webb advocates for an internet in which "AI systems explicitly mitigate against gender bias." She calls us all to action: "In accepting the internet as something built for us by big tech corporations, we've given up some of our control....We have to take our power back. And we have to get our voices back. And together we have to create an internet where no one is left behind."[28]

FIG 39. HOW DOES AI AUGMENT HUMAN RELATIONSHIPS? Interaction design studio Hyphen-Labs commissioned Comuzi to contribute to their technology and power exhibition at the Tate Exchange, Tate Modern. The resulting workshop asked participants to consider the role of AI in shaping relationships with others and then to prototype speculative AI artifacts that could potentially augment human relationships in 2029.

"All data is inherently human. There's nothing cold or mechanical about data. It needs to be handled with care."—Caroline Sinders

In addition to adjusting data points, individuals should be able to query algorithmic systems in other ways. Sinders suggests opening these systems to external audits of code releases, datasets, the age of the model, etc. She envisions an open-source mentality around AI that will make the tech accessible and accountable to those using it—a human-rights centered design approach that respects a user's privacy and data.[29] Also an advocate of algorithmic transparency, Adam Cutler, Distinguished Designer at IBM Design, maintains that we need standards around AI similar to those of nutrition labels.[30] Of course, nutrition labels themselves are notoriously hard to understand.[31] They assume a certain level of preexisting knowledge around dietary language and recommendations. Designing AI in a clear, understandable way raises similar issues of topic literacy.

Quite a few designers are helping nonexperts grow familiar with AI so that they might knowledgeably respond to automated systems. Alex Fefegha, founder of Comuzi studios, along with colleagues Akil Benjamin and Sekyeong Kwon, created the AI Cheatsheet site to help nonexperts. The site defines twenty key AI terms using plain language, each with a maximum of 140 characters, and then explains to the public how AI affects everyday life.[32] [Fig. 37]. Comuzi has worked on numerous projects that engage community members with AI, including a collaboration with Dr. Charlotte Webb of the Feminist Internet, a collective working "to make the internet a more equal space for women and other marginalized groups through creative, critical practice."[33] [Fig. 38] Webb worked with Fefegha to create F'xa, a "feminist guide to AI bias." This playful chatbot converses with individuals about bias by channeling diverse perspectives. Such projects elevate AI literacy in community members, giving people the vocabulary and conceptual understanding needed to talk back to the technology.

HUMAN RIGHTS-CENTERED DESIGN: a design process that focuses on supporting in the technological realm the same kinds of human rights typically advocated for in civil society

Artist and researcher Mimi Onuoha came together with artist, DJ, and educator Mother Cyborg, to take on AI literacy as well. According to Mother Cyborg, the two women noticed that "there were specific groups talking about AI, but the groups that would be affected were not in the room."[34] To correct this, they worked with designers to create *The People's Guide to AI*, a friendly AI zine/workbook informed by sound pedagogical methods. As Mother Cyborg explains, they created "an analogue touchstone for those afraid of the digital world, putting technical knowledge in the hands of the people who have been socialized to believe they are not and could never be 'technologists.'"[35]

PEDAGOGICAL: anything concerned with teaching

Frustratingly, designers often have an easier time convincing communities than companies of the value of helping individuals understand automated decisions. Designers have difficulty establishing how such transparent decision-making features translate into greater user productivity and bigger sales.[36] The tendency for companies to make predictive algorithms proprietary also constructs barriers against widespread user knowledge. Some companies buy ML systems and use them out of the box with little understanding themselves of the logic behind them.[37] This ignorance is particularly dangerous when companies purchase a proprietary system made for one industry and apply it to another.[38] Designers need both the expertise and the gumption to point out to industry that automated systems can't be improved if people—individuals or companies—can't get to the meat to understand how they work.

Designing transparent interactions for users will require honing new skills for designers. Product teams often ask designers to take the output of AI experts, like data scientists, and translate that output into useful insights for nonexperts. Accurately portraying such insights requires that the designer carefully communicate the model's limitations, the uncertainty behind a model's predictions. Rumman Chowdhury, founder of Parity, advises that designers always ask experts to articulate those limitations. She explains, "Frankly, the answer should not be that there are no limitations. It's literally a model. It's a representation. It's the same as a model airplane or model car. It's not perfect. I would always ask what the shortcomings are, where it could fall apart, and then think through how you might highlight that uncertainty to the end user."[39]

What does Chowdhury mean by uncertainty? She asks us to imagine that a judge is using an AI system to decide if someone gets bail. The AI model would score someone, perhaps from zero to one. Based on the score, a perpetrator might be placed in a green (yes), yellow (maybe), or red (no) bucket. Some people, according to the model, might fall firmly in one of these three categories. But many people would land on the edges. How does the interface communicate to the judge which people, for example, fell in the red bucket, rather than the yellow bucket, because of a difference of only .1 percent? Chowdhury explains, "The biggest thing to think about in designing this translation is information fidelity—how do you retain the information about the uncertainty in a way so that an end user can take intelligent action?"[40] Would you want to remain in prison because of a difference of .1 percent? Would you want to be denied medical care? Denied a loan? If designers don't communicate the limitations of the models, users can't question automated decisions—decisions that can have a critical impact on many individuals' lives. Such uncertainty could be communicated through data visualizations, interaction patterns, conversational interface, virtual agents, etc. Working in this area provides huge opportunities for designers to positively impact the integration of ML into the decision-making process.[41]

YOU AREN'T MANIPULATING ME...

ML systems depend on data—your data. If an interface or service doesn't know who you are—or at least what profile bucket in which to put you—it can't create a positive user experience that responds to your needs. Based on your past behavior, should the system classify you as someone likely to

> *"The perfection of machine learning can hinder us. And the imperfection of humans might be a benefit."*
> —Molly Wright Steenson, Carnegie Mellon University

read *Little Fires Everywhere*? Likely to march with Antifa? Likely to buy an air fryer? Likely to develop adult-onset diabetes? Individual names are less important than the ability to match you to a specific behavior profile. And these profiles become more and more comprehensive as your data is bought and sold between companies by professional data brokers.

How is this data collected? Dozens of third-party trackers follow a user's every move online. These trackers can even archive text that individuals type but delete before sharing.[42] Sensors can biometrically identify people via their gait, their heartbeat, their fingerprints, or their iris patterns, not just up close but from a distance. Or they can use your license plate, your credit card info, your phone number, the MAC address broadcast from your smartphone and picked up over Wi-Fi or Bluetooth, even your own face.[43]

This constant flow of unregulated, cross-pollinating data produces a system of mass surveillance. But you may argue, what's wrong with mass surveillance? I don't need privacy. Only bad people doing bad things need privacy. Journalist Glenn Greenwald references this attitude in his talk "Why Privacy Matters."[44] Despite what people claim, he maintains, everyone wants some degree of privacy. We say things to our partner, for example, that we wouldn't say to our boss. We don't give out passwords to our private accounts willy-nilly. In addition, "our behavior changes when we think we are being watched…. There are dozens of psychological studies that prove that when someone knows they might be watched, the behavior they engage in is vastly more conformist and compliant." That's why tyrants love surveillance and free societies do not. Most importantly, Greenwald explains, "It is a realm of privacy…in which creativity and exploration and dissent exclusively reside." As creative people advocating for humans, we designers should have a particularly strong stake in protecting private spaces.[45]

FIG 40. A PEOPLE'S GUIDE TO AI. Mimi Onuoha and Diana J. Nucera (a.k.a. Mother Cyborg) worked with the studio And Also Too to create this beginner's guide to AI. The resulting zine, paired with a series of community workshops, opens up AI to individuals from a range of backgrounds, suggesting that each person can contribute to an equitable technological future.

FIG 41. IDENTIFYING EMOTIONS FROM WALKING USING AFFECTIVE AND DEEP FEATURES. In 2019, researchers from the University of North Carolina and the University of Maryland—Tanmay Randhavane, Uttaran Bhattacharya, Kyra Kapsaskis, Kurt Gray, Aniket Bera, and Dinesh Manocha—created a novel data-driven model that uses gait features to classify a human's perceived emotional state as happy, sad, angry, or neutral. Such projects raise interesting questions around the correlation of the body with emotion, as well as potential avenues of surveillance around emotional expression.

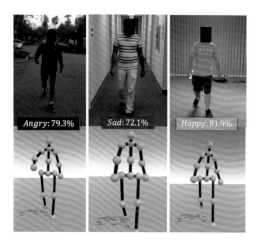

FIG 42. PROBABLY CHELSEA. Installation view of *A Becoming Resemblance*, featuring *Probably Chelsea* (2017). Artist and biohacker Heather Dewey-Hagborg analyzed Chelsea Manning's DNA using a single hair and then algorithmically generated thirty different possible portraits, none of which are actually Manning. Her work raises questions around surveillance and the body, particularly the limitations of the technology. According to Dewey-Hagborg, soon after she completed her project, a for-profit company created similar technology to be used by police, further entangling her own project in critical issues of today. [46]

FIG 43. *HIGHER RESOLUTION*. The Tate Exchange commissioned Hyphen-Labs, a collective of engineers, architects, designers, and artists led by Ece Tankal and Carmen Aguilar y Wedge, to curate this exhibition around ML, privacy, behavior, and digital rights. The project, a collaboration with design researcher Caroline Sinders, as well as numerous artists and speakers, encourages visitors to converse in physical spaces within the exhibition—the park bench, the living room, the loo—as metaphors for exploring expectations and rights around digital privacy. In one of the installations called *Likepad* (top right), Hyphen-Labs collaborated with Random Happiness to enable users to leave a "physical like" with their fingerprint in their environment.

We can begin to see how privacy relates to personal liberty, innovation, and creativity. What other dangers might trackers and sensors introduce? Let's go back to the data. In chapter two we discussed how the introduction of context-aware data collection will better inform algorithmic systems, resulting in more intelligent, unobtrusive interactions with machines—from doctors learning of potential clinical trials while they converse with patients to kids learning the physics behind a ball they are throwing.[47]

But, as Maes points out: the big challenge is how to monitor context in a way that protects people's privacy... especially when the context starts to include data about our physiology, like a rising heart rate or electrodermal activity, which is a measure of excitement."[48] Big data is broadening to include insight into actions, emotions, and even thoughts, in response to the surrounding digital—even physical—environment. In other words, insight into what makes you you. This knowledge can produce thoughtful, engaging designs, but it can also manipulate populations, a problem that will intensify as we capture more context to correlate with more data points.

The now-infamous story of Cambridge Analytica brought this danger to the attention of the public in 2018. Cambridge Analytica collected the data of more than fifty million people via an online personality quiz conducted through Facebook. The firm, who worked for the Trump campaign, then used these data points to construct profiles of Americans and target them with persuasive ads in the 2016 presidential election.[49] David Carroll, an associate professor of media design at the New School's Parsons School of Design, played a key role in the subsequent outing and bankruptcy of Cambridge Analytica, when he filed a legal claim requesting to see the data points of his own profile. According to Europe's General Data Protection Regulation (GDPR), enacted in 2018, Europeans have "the right to request and delete their data, and requir[e] businesses to receive informed consent before collecting that data."[50] In addition to personal data, European citizens can even request "the inferences and predictions that machines make about us."[51] Carroll leveraged this law to make his case.

As a result of Cambridge Analytica and other data scandals, particularly around social media platforms and large technology companies, Americans are growing aware that privacy is under threat.[52] Globally, this issue takes center stage as well, as demonstrated by the Chinese Social Credit System, a mass surveillance system that allows the government to consolidate information on individual Chinese citizens and then punish or reward them based on the resulting score.[53] Designers in China, and, perhaps, right here in the US, have collaborated with governments to design such systems. As noted by Bruce Schneier, a fellow at the Harvard Kennedy School, "In countries like China, a surveillance infrastructure is being built by the government for social control. In countries like the US, it's being built by corporations in order to influence our buying behavior, and is incidentally used by the government."[54]

Social psychologist Shoshana Zuboff, professor emerita at Harvard Business School, frames this threat as "surveillance capitalism." She explains, "Capitalism has always worked by claiming things that live outside the marketplace—like innocent forests and mountain sides and rivers and fields—and dragging them into the market dynamic, turning them into commodities that can be sold and purchased....Google discovered what may be the last virgin wood. That turns out to be our private experience. Google claimed private experience as free raw material to be translated into behavioral data." Today, she asserts, "the market capitalization of Microsoft, Google, Facebook, and Amazon depend on the revenues that flow through these [behavioral futures markets]."[55]

"Surveillance capitalism," she warns, "operates through unprecedented asymmetries in knowledge and the power that accrues to knowledge. Surveillance capitalists know everything *about us*, whereas their operations are designed to be unknowable *to us*. They accumulate vast domains of new knowledge

"If, however, you want to retain some control over your personal existence and the future of life, you have to run faster than the algorithms, faster than Amazon and the government, and get to know yourself before they do."—Yuval Noah Harari, Hebrew University of Jerusalem

from us, but not *for us*. They predict our futures for the sake of others' gains, not ours."[56] Looking ahead, Zuboff warns, surveillance capitalism is on a collision course with democracy because "in order to get…predictions that approximate certainty, it must interfere with human autonomy, with our agency, with our ability to decide what I do now and what I do next."[57] Douglas Rushkoff cautions us of this kind of manipulation, as well, in his book *Team Human* in which he writes that algorithms "engage with the data we leave in our wake to make assumptions about who we are and how we will behave. Then they push us to behave more consistently with what they have determined to be our statistically most probable selves. They want us to be true to our profiles."[58]

DARK INTERACTION PATTERNS: deceptive user interactions designed to mislead or trick users into doing something they might not want to do

So what can designers do about all of this? If algorithmically driven behavioral modification does threaten our autonomy—even our democracy—what role can design play to put us back on track? How can data be gathered responsibly so that humans can benefit from ML systems while protecting the privacy of individuals? How can designers help shore up user knowledge and agency even as third parties quietly abscond with data behind the facade of our lovely designed interfaces?

To answer, we first need to understand what's standing in the way of individuals controlling their own data right now. In the US, blanket permissions and dark interaction patterns work against data rights. Blanket permissions ask users to opt in or opt out, with few possibilities in between. Opt in and you can stream music, access software, track your fitness level. Opt out and lose it all. The opt in function takes very little effort, i.e., individuals are often automatically opted in. The opt out function, on the other hand, requires multiple steps. Dark

FIG 44. DATA PATTERNS. This collection, cataloged by IF, a studio founded by Sarah Gold, shares a range of interaction design patterns to help creative teams address ethical issues around collecting and using people's data. Themes in the patterns engage with actions such as authentication, encryption, contextual access, activity logs, masking data, and one-time access.

Understanding automated decisions [3]

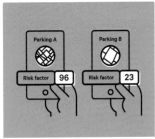

Decision testing

Notice of upcoming action

Activity log

Giving access to data [6]

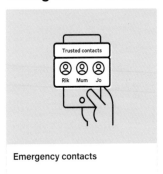

Emergency contacts

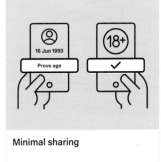

Minimal sharing

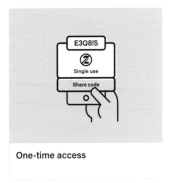

One-time access

Giving and removing consent [7]

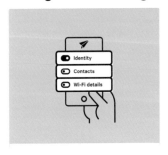

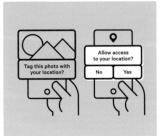

interaction patterns can intentionally trick the user into selecting unintended options or overlooking detailed options around data use.[59] European interfaces provide a model for providing more granular choices around data, choices insured by the GDPR. However, even in Europe dark patterns frequently appear as an insidious response to legislated data protections.[60] Such patterns highlight the high impact of interface design upon data choice—whether used to confuse users or elucidate rights.

So how can designers help hand control of data back to the people? Legislators are already proposing similar digital rights regulation in the US. Legally granting individuals options around data usage in a manner similar to the GDPR is necessary but not enough. Such legislation is meaningless if the resulting data choices are not apparent and actionable to users. Carefully designed interfaces can articulate these choices, along with context on how the data will be shared.[61] In coming years the ability of designers to successfully create such interactions will be incredibly important. To support such digital rights, for example, designers can raise user-experience questions, such as, "Is the user able to make data choices at appropriate moments in the task flow?" "Are these choices engaging or tedious?" "Are potential paths of action confusing or empowering?" "Can the user dig into the interface to get more information?" "Can the user trace data usage both in the moment and beyond the initial share?"

For example, terms of service agreements often communicate rights around privacy and data in digital spaces. Although these, in theory, protect the user, companies actually write these long, drawn out, verbally obtuse agreements to protect themselves with no expectations of customer reads. How could designers, instead, as Gold suggests, put "the information about when services are learning, what data is being used, and what powers a user has to change that—all at a point of use?"[62] How could designers serve up quick, relevant tidbits, easily read and acted upon? Her technology studio IF provides

TASK FLOW: a series of steps that users must move through to complete a specific task

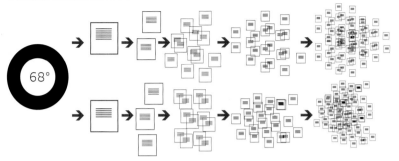

a robust catalog of interaction patterns with such questions in mind. This catalog supports agency-inducing interactions, such as "Just-in-time Consent," "Masking Personal Data," and much more. [Fig. 44] Scaffolding best practice like this provides needed support to help designers back individuals' digital rights.[63]

But even with such quick, intuitive interaction patterns, protecting data privacy grows ever more complex due to sheer volume. Back in 2016, researchers Guido Noto La Diega and Ian Walden found that if you add together all the legal notices associated with Nest thermostats, "a thousand [privacy] contracts may apply!"[64] Who can peruse a thousand contacts? How can individuals pragmatically protect their data when they can barely keep up with their email inbox? And, even if permissions are carefully granted, who actually has time to follow up and make sure companies are respecting their choices around data?[65]

One solution might be to create AI to monitor AI. Consider, for example, virtual personal privacy assistants. Seattle design studio Artefact prototyped a virtual agent named Kagi, who could "work in the background, quietly monitoring app activity to make sure no questionable decisions are being made without the user's consent." Artefact acknowledges that building trust in an agent like this will take time, but they envision that "protect[ing] data from automatic access" will enable users to "monetize or extract value from their data in new ways."[66] [Fig. 45]

Other virtual privacy assistants have popped up in recent years. Professor Norman Sadeh, who leads the Personalized Privacy Assistant Project at Carnegie Mellon University, looks specifically at data privacy issues around the internet of things (IoT). He notes that the situation grows even more difficult when there is no screen through which data preferences can be selected. The embedded nature of IoT devices make third-party data capture quite invisible and the need for something like a personal privacy assistant to navigate user privacy more essential.[67]

Others—e.g., design researchers, legislators—suggest that we need official government or nonprofit organizations to represent individual data rights in the face of conflicting private industry goals.[68] Gold refers to this as "methods of collective consent." She proposes that such organizations can act in the best interest of consumers, navigating privacy issues for individuals but also helping the larger society "course correct." Imagine a Better Business Bureau or a union to collectively bargain for data rights. In concert with personal privacy agents, large advocacy organizations could compile data from multiple consumers to identify and respond to patterns of data rights abuse.[69] Such organizations could leverage these patterns to identify critical points of intervention.

ML oversight, whether provided by a combination of legislation, personal privacy agents, representative organizations, or other approaches, in the end, could work toward everyone's best interest. Chowdhury argues that such oversight will not only move society toward a more just future, but also encourage leaps forward in the ML space. She explains: "Brakes help a car go faster. If we have the right kinds of guard rails to tell us if something is going to get out of control, we feel more comfortable taking risks."[70] Designers can help build those guard rails. We can create beautiful, efficient systems that camouflage automated injustice, or we can be the eyes that peer into the system and share knowledge back to the people. Individuals need the tools to demand intelligent systems worthy of their trust—and we can build those tools.

INTERNET OF THINGS (IOT): network that connects physical objects with the internet via embedded sensors, software, and other technologies

"Humans work within institutions. AI systems don't have any of these systems around them to hold them accountable. But we could build them."—Kate Crawford, AI Now Institute, NYU

IN SUM: DON'T THROW UP YOUR HANDS. TAKE ACTION.

It is easy to be overwhelmed and, subsequently, paralyzed by the immense need for ML ethics. Algorithmic systems reflect and amplify existing societal bias. Narrow, biased training data provides one example of this in action. The very act of classification problematically validates some categories while negating others. Sensors gather data via human bodies, effectively erasing anyone who doesn't physically fit typical parameters. Until interfaces clearly communicate the logic behind algorithmic decision making, users will not be able to hold these systems accountable. Designers and the communities they serve need to understand digital rights. The unregulated flow of personal data leads to manipulation of individuals. Americans are growing aware of the threat that invasive data harvesting poses to our democratic society. Through the design of interactions, designers can articulate digital rights and guide users toward options, or we can trick them into giving data away. We can work to break complex privacy agreements into quick, comprehensible, just-in-time interactions. We can prototype future-facing concepts, like personal privacy agents, and support collective digital rights organizations. We can hold ourselves and industry accountable for the choices we carve out for individuals through our designs. We can let ML prey on those our society already victimizes, or we can use the technology as a mechanism for equity and justice.

DATA HARVESTING: a process through which a script automatically extracts—or scrapes—large quantities of data online to use for other purposes, sometimes nefarious

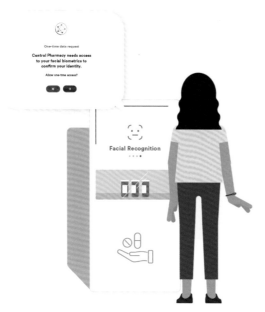

FIG 45. KAGI. Designers at Artefact prototyped this personal privacy advocate to manage an individual's data preferences in lieu of direct action by the user. The virtual agent would get to know the user's preferences over time, while navigating thousands of discrete data privacy policies to act in the best interest of the user.

FIG 46. PENNY. Designers from Stamen Design worked with researchers from Carnegie Mellon University to train an AI to predict the income level of an area based on satellite imagery. They built the system on top of GBDX, DigitalGlobe's analytics platform. The resulting tool enables users to adjust imagery—green spaces, parking lots, buildings, etc.—to gain insight into the AI's decision-making process, thus breaking down the Black Box Problem.

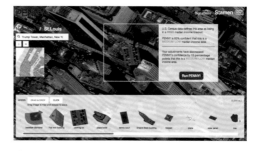

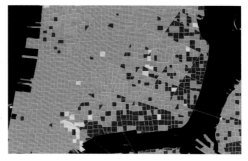

RUMMAN CHOWDHURY, PHD
Interview

A practicing data scientist and artificial intelligence (AI) developer, Rumman Chowdhury holds degrees in quantitative social science. Dr. Chowdhury is the CEO and founder of Parity, a company dedicated to creating ethical AI software. She was formerly the global lead for responsible AI at Accenture Applied Intelligence, working with C-suite clients to create technical solutions for ethical, explainable, and transparent AI.

What design ethics issues should designers be concerned about?

There's so much, especially when we think about artificial intelligence. There is an important role to be played in how you translate statistical output or quantitative output or an AI output into something understandable by the person at the end of the chain, who is often the least knowledgeable person about statistics or AI. That design component is how that information is shared or not shared. It's how we illustrate our values and how we prioritize what is important to us. I'll give you one example: The design of dating apps gears you toward images, and if it gears you toward images, what are you assessing people on but on how they look? The design component tells people to prioritize appearance over all else because what do you do? You look at a picture, and you swipe left and you swipe right. If we think about that, there is an algorithm behind that; there is a model that was built to say, "Here are the people you're most compatible with." It was designed ultimately to say, "We've curated these people for you, but you've got to pick the one you think is hot." Physically hot, not intellectually compatible, not emotionally—physically hot—because that's what we're putting in front of you.

How can designers take action in these circumstances?

I've mentioned translating uncertainty. The second arsenal you have in your tool kit is giving the end user some agency. So how might the person on the end not just be the recipient of an output but also be an active participant in maybe highlighting flaws or, you know, improving how it works or thinking of this as something iterative and cyclical? How can we build this in a way that respects and preserves human judgment at the same level that algorithmic judgment is often respected? Just think about the power dynamic of the individual using the thing that has been built. Is the technology running the person, or is the person running the technology? I wrote an article called "The Retrofit Human," about how we optimize technology and then we expect human beings to shape themselves around technology. The example I give is the self-driving car. Originally, what was pitched to us—and what we all imagined—was that we would take a nap in a car while it drove itself. Everyone's like, wow, that's going to reduce congestion in cities. More people will move to the suburbs. And then slowly, as that veil was taken away, we realized the limitations of the technology. Now a self-driving car is a car—though your hands aren't on the wheel, you still have to do all the stressful things, like constantly pay attention and hold all the liability. You still have to do the work. It's supplementary.

It's not what we were sold. What tech companies are saying is: human beings, you have to adjust to the limitations of our technology instead of seeing it the other way around. And all of this is rooted in techno-narcissism, or what Meredith Broussard calls *technochauvinism*, in Silicon Valley—the notion that human beings are flawed and technology will save us.

This fundamental belief that the technology is always better than the human often falls apart, most often in edge cases. And edge cases tend to be vulnerable communities. Edge cases tend to be, by definition, not the majority; therefore, they are a minority. Unsurprisingly, if your technology falls apart in edge cases, who are these edge cases but the people who are already the most marginalized and discriminated against?

I love that image of the car because who wants to be the person who has all of the stress but can't put their hands on the wheel?
Right. And none of the agency. So what we've done is completely remove the only part about driving that some people find enjoyable, which is the driving, and then kept all the stress. So you think of the Uber self-driving car example where it hit that pedestrian, and ultimately, people were playing a game of hot potato with the liability. They were looking at the woman who was the driver, the test driver. Wait, hold on. What's the point of self-driving cars, then, except to make a few people really rich?

It did nothing for humanity. And also, by the way, people are talking about, oh, actually, the problem with self-driving cars is that roads and cities aren't built the right way. So, again, we want to reshape society because it's not fitting the technological dream that we have. It is baffling.

What other advice do you have for designers working with machine learning?
You actually hold power and agency. Don't defer to the programmer. They are just another person in the pipeline. They don't hold more power than you. They are not smarter than you. They are not better than you. And you have an expertise that they do not, even if they don't respect it. You have the ability and the right, frankly, as a person in this chain of command, to shape things in the way that you think is positive.

DAVID CARROLL
Interview

An associate professor of media design at Parsons School of Design at the New School, David Carroll engages in research that advocates for digital rights while surfacing issues around data privacy. As featured in the film *The Great Hack* on Netflix, Carroll legally challenged Cambridge Analytica to reveal his 2016 voter profile thus raising critical issues around data harvesting, data insights, and behavior manipulation.

Excerpt from interview with Lee-Sean Huang, AIGA, March 18, 2020.

DC: We used to talk about privacy. Now we're talking about data rights. Changing the words is significant. We've made a considerable stride in that regard because *privacy* is a meaningless word. A privacy policy is really a surveillance policy.

When a company says they care about your privacy—but they never define what that means—this gets to the underlying challenge.

This brings us to the question of whether we should have the right to sell our personal data or whether that's really the question we should be asking at all. One of the other subjects in *The Great Hack*, Brittany Kaiser, has espoused a property rights perspective to data. This perspective comes from her frustration at how hard it is to enforce human rights, especially in the United States. We're good at regulating property rights, and so there's a natural gravity to think that way. And, of course, the industry would love this, too, because they don't want to interrupt the business model.

However, when you think about it more critically, you realize that moving toward property rights and being able to sell your data probably makes the situation a hundred times worse because then you get to the point where everyone is in a compulsory arrangement to sell. Data is not like real estate. It can be copied an infinite number of times. How do you really control it?

I've not seen a technical model or implementation that would actually enable people to sell their data. And that data—personal data—is relatively worthless. It is valuable in aggregate. It is valuable to train models and algorithms that then don't even need the original data.

There are a lot of flaws in the notion of treating data like property even though it sounds good on paper. Data as a civil right or a human right is more in line with the European model, and there's a lot to be said for adopting a global standard. In that sense, it's about setting limits and restrictions, which industry is not going to like; but, unfortunately, I think we need to start saying no to things.

LSH: Saying no sounds like a system-wide policy decision and a political struggle that we have to work on. I'd love to get your take on how we design these products and interfaces. Do you have thoughts about how we move toward data transparency through either better interfaces or relationships with the apps that we use?

DC: This was the crux of my lawsuit against Cambridge Analytica. In the UK, I had transparency rights—the company had to disclose the contents of my profile. In addition to that I had the right to have it explained to me. The company refused to abide by its legal obligations to explain. This was upheld by the regulator there—the data protection authority—i.e. the information commissioner's office. They seized Cambridge Analytica servers under criminal warrant and convicted the company for refusing to give me my data, because of this legal obligation.

So, there are still legal battles that need to be fought over achieving what's written in the books, i.e., that companies, at least in Europe, have to explain when you ask. And if they can't explain, that's a problem.

The other interesting thing about the European model is that inferred data is considered personal data, so the inferences and predictions that machines make about us belong to us. As soon as they are attached to our name, we have rights to them there. In the US, we don't have this. If you listened to Mark Zuckerberg speaking to Congress, he insisted that users have control of their data, but his definition of that is he gives back to us the data we gave to Facebook, if we want it. He's not giving us the inferences that he and Facebook are creating about us using that data.

There are a lot more legal fights that have to happen to give us rights to our data, the inferences, and the explanations. That will challenge the business of algorithms because algorithms are not naturally able to tell us why. They can be accurate, but even the people who write them aren't totally sure why. This is because machine learning and artificial intelligence is an alien brain. As humans, we cannot necessarily contemplate how it thinks. Machine learning thinks in multidimensional space, as many dimensions as necessary to model out the outcomes. Whereas humans are pretty limited to thinking in three dimensions.

This is a problem of continuing to outsource much of humanity to this alien brain. We don't have the legal strength in place to force algorithms to explain themselves to us even though that will better ensure that we have a more equitable relationship with them.

The Cambridge Analytica story runs deeper than it appears. The conversation illuminates many of the core issues with which we'll continue to wrestle.

CAROLINE SINDERS
Interview

Founder of the agency Convocation Design + Research, Caroline Sinders examines technology's impact in society, interface design, AI, abuse, and politics in digital, conversational spaces. As a machine-learning-design researcher and artist, she's worked with Amnesty International, Intel, IBM Watson, the Wikimedia Foundation, and others.

You've said that to create with AI, we need human rights–centered design. Can you speak a bit about the difference between human-centered design and human rights–centered design?

If we look at the history, human-centered design was monumental and recentered how software was made. But human-centered design has reached its limits, in terms of pushing designers to think beyond their own experiences. We have to confront those limitations right now in our practice. When designers are thinking of personas or users, we grab onto things that are too comfortable. We're thinking of maybe our friends or just our community. We're in a global community now. When designers make things, those things are put out in the world—lots of people are using them. It's time to take that human-centered design foundation and add a lot more scaffolding onto it. It's time to iterate on top of it—that's where human rights–centered design comes in.

The crux of this design approach is taking human rights policy and conversations that are happening in civil society—that policymakers and researchers and technologists have been shouting from the rafters—and recognizing that those conversations need to affect technology now. A bunch of us came up with the term around 2016, but it gained popularity in the human rights world in 2019. So now, a line in the sand, it's 2020. We need to be designing with this in mind.

It's easy to be overwhelmed by all the problems associated with machine-learning—bias, surveillance, personal security, agency. You're taking on these pervasive problems through positive actions. Do you have any advice for designers who also want to take this kind of decisive action?

Privacy and security seem daunting, but the more you bring it into your practice, the easier it gets. It becomes second nature to say, "Oh, wait, how are we going to store that?" "What kind of encryption are we going to use?" "Did we set aside a budget for encrypting and securing the database?" "Okay, let's make sure we tell people." Start to bring in questions around privacy, security, and bias in the beginning of your process.

So I'd like to talk about your project the Feminist Data Set. This project has a strong participatory component. What does community engagement have to do with the generation of datasets?

There should be more community driven datasets. The initial seeds of the Feminist Data Set were from when I recognized my own limitations as a person. I have bias. I'm only aware of so many experiences. Why don't I lean into the great people around me and have a large diversity of different kinds of texts? I need to let go of control and open it up to people. There are so many interesting humans in the world. If someone is interested in coming to a workshop that's about feminist data, they may have a lot to contribute.

Yet it strikes me that your workshops are changing our understanding of data and data sets. Even while the workshops create alternative data sets, they can go on to transform the process in which we see these data sets.

It's farm-to-table data. Artisanal data. I call it the slow data movement. A product I would love to do in New Orleans is a slow data project with a neighborhood to think through mapping that neighborhood—what it would mean and how could the neighborhood be in control of that data. I'm interested in things like that. I see Feminist Data Set as a part of a growing practice.

As a part of the Feminist Data Set project, you mentioned that you may write a different type of natural language processing algorithms to analyze language as a protest against inequality. Can you talk about that?

As you know, natural language processing is the kind of algorithm I'll be using to analyze the text in the project. We may have to build something. I'm not sure what that will look like or entail, but it's something that my collaborator Hannah Davis and I have to work through. I was inspired by Aylin Caliskan, a Turkish researcher who noted gender bias in Google Translate.

There seems to be a general feeling right now around AI that we're in a critical moment. And there's a lot of tension and fear around that. Do you think this is true?

I think so, but more around product design and consumer products. There is such an emphasis on bias, which is important. But I don't see a lot of oversight of how products use artificial intelligence. That's a lot of what I try to advocate for or have deeper conversations around. We can't propel criticism forward if we leave designers out of the mix. They're the ones making and designing and thinking about these products. This is where a human rights–centered design framework comes into play—things that help designers other than just ethics guidelines, things they can actually use, like actual examples and workshops and personas. So when designers release something, society isn't the quality assurance tester. We are in a critical moment to move design to the forefront of this conversation.

SARAH GOLD
Interview

Sarah Gold is founder and CEO of IF, a technology studio specializing in ethical and practical uses of data. Leveraging her interest in privacy, security, and systems change, Gold creates interventions that explore how technology can respect more of our rights.

Why do you think designers should care about machine learning right now?

It's important for designers to realize how political their work is. The digital technologies that designers are involved in creating are now among the biggest distributors of powers and capabilities in society. In some ways, the digital technologies that we use indicate our capacity for participating in citizenship—being part of a society. Designers have great power in deciding what features are included in particular products. These features might, for example, provide a form of redress or the ability to participate in what a product does or how far it might stretch into their lives.

Machine learning is where technology is going next. Organizations have access to more information about more people than ever before. Data represents people. This isn't information about something that doesn't matter, this is about our lives and our future. Machine-learning technologies can be used on top of that data to

help designers or product owners make decisions or give insights to politicians. If we don't know how machine learning works, we can't interrogate why it works a particular way. We can't bring what we do best as designers: facilitate conversations between different practitioners to find insights about issues that are dense or difficult to talk about. And we can't begin to advocate for change in a creative way where we're looking at what's possible. That's important when we know that the data that has been captured historically and—even today—is inherently discriminatory. I do think it's part of the designers' responsibility to understand the biases that they are working with and then assess and shape the outputs so that they bring more equitable futures rather than increasingly discriminatory ones.

You've spoken in the past about this idea of creating representational organizations when individuals don't have the time or the knowledge to take on these systems deeply. Can you talk about that idea a little bit?

This is one of the trade-offs that we need to think about as designers: information overload is real. Decision fatigue is real. We feel that every day. And so do the people that we're designing for. We often find that

"How can you grant a user the 'right to understand' in a world that is nondeterministic without overwhelming them?"—Sarah Gold

people have little time to do the interrogation themselves or do their due diligence, which maybe they otherwise would want to have done but might not have the skills to do it. There are lots of people for whom using technology products is a hard and scary thing to do. It's our responsibility to make sure we don't leave those people out.

Let's say, twenty years from now, we live in a society in which individuals do have more agency over their own data and do have systems in place to help them maneuver that complexity. Can you describe what that kind of interaction might look like?
The type of work I'm excited about is around collective action for data. At IF, we are currently calling this "methods of collective consent." What are the ways that you can encourage people to participate in how individual data could be used that supports public interest—alongside verifiable transparency? How can the type of software we use on top of datasets create assurance about how data has been used? That is quite a shift away from what we have at the moment, which is you have to consent to how data is used and then just trust that we're going to use it appropriately, and if we get found out, we'll put an email out and apologize and get fined. Instead, I believe we need continuous monitoring and assurance

about how data is used. That assurance could be provided by new organizations or representatives.

It could be an organization whose values you align with in regard to a particular part of your life. It could be that those organizations actually are automated elements. It's entirely possible to see small agents or an AI acting on our behalf and negotiating some of that digital social-contract space on our behalf. Some of this might be automated, some of it might be more traditional work done in person.

The experience would include signing up to one or more of those representatives to whom you would delegate decision making on your behalf based on values that you've set. For anything that sits outside the original data consent that you've given, you then have this participatory process to be able to agree or disagree as to whether that is something that you'd be okay with happening. In some ways there are examples of this already with workers' unions where you have organizations that operate on your behalf. But I think that we need allyship in our digital lives as well because it's becoming far more complex—bigger and harder to manage in many ways.

What Is Missing Is Still There
Mimi Ọnụọha

A Nigerian American artist and researcher, Ọnụọha highlights in her work the social relationships and power dynamics behind data collection. Her multimedia practice uses print, code, installation, and video to call attention to the ways in which those in the margins are differently abstracted, represented, and missed by sociotechnical systems.

My interest in missing things began with what I could see. For a long time, I have kept a small piece of paper taped to the bottom right corner of my desk. This paper comes and goes, at times becoming wrinkled, discolored by tea stains, or hidden under a stack of books. But it always serves the same purpose: listing the most eccentric datasets that I can find online.

Before the score and lyrics for the hit American musical *Hamilton* had been released, a group of obsessed fans created a shared document of every word in the show. This dataset made my list. In 2016, a Reddit user published a post with a link to where he had downloaded the metadata of every story ever published on fanfiction.net, a popular site for stories about fandoms. This, too, made the list.

Other things that have graced the list: the daily count of footballs produced by the Wilson Sporting Goods football factory in Ada, Iowa (4,000 as of 2008); an estimation of the number of hot dogs eaten by Americans on the Fourth of July every year (most recently: 150 million); the locations of every public toilet in Australia (of which there are more than 17,000).

Australian academic Mitchell Whitelaw defines data as measurements extracted from the flux of the real. When we typically think of collecting data, we think of big, important things: census information, UN data about health and diseases, data mined by large companies like Google, Amazon, or Facebook.

"Statistics want to simplify and life wants to complicate."
—Mimi Onụọha

From this perspective Whitelaw's definition of data is admirably concise and effective. With its clever use of the word *extraction*, it hints at the resource-driven nature of data collection. Like Shoshana Zuboff's concept of surveillance capitalism, which describes our modern ascendance into a form of capitalism that monetizes data gathered through perfunctory surveillance, Whitelaw's definition calls to mind corporate imaginings of data as a resource. In a capitalist society, it is always a smart business decision to collect data. A world collected is a world classified is a world rendered legible is a world made profitable.

But when I glance at the list on my desk, it is not always easy to spot the direct line that connects the datasets to the concepts of resource extraction and omnipresent surveillance. While less conventional, those datasets are also vertices of quantification, facts extracted from surprising corners of reality. And so a simpler definition comes to mind.

Data: the things that we measure and care about.

This is the beauty I find in the list of odd data on my desk. If Whitelaw's definition suggests a world that is pure source, a heap of raw material waiting to be cut up and structured into neat cells and Excel spreadsheets, then mine highlights the opposite: the fact that all datasets are created by people who have a stake in their creation.

The corollary is also true. If we wish to know more about what our societies, corporations, and communities value, we should simply look to what data is collected. The things we measure are the things we care about.

When I first began creating my list of weird data, I wasn't sure why I was doing it. Idle curiosity seemed the most obvious reason, and fascination with novel forms of procrastination another.

But at some point, the answer became clear to me. When it did, I added an additional item to the piece of paper. This item was a quote, taken from an old conversation that I had had with a former colleague.

"Humans make sense of the world through exclusion."

The quote came from John Fass, a fellow researcher from the Royal College of Art, whose work focused on design and interfaces. John and I had been talking in the empty canteen one day, when he offhandedly mentioned that he considered exclusion to be a crucial aspect of design.

The only way that humans were able to make sense of the world, he insisted, was by sifting through information and making decisions about what needed to be excluded at any given time. Narratives only work because of the many mundane details that are removed in the course of their telling. In a sense, all stories we tell ourselves are exercises in leaving things out.

It was not the first time I had heard this concept, but on that day it resonated with me. In their seminal (and very dry) academic text *Sorting Things Out,* Geoffrey Bowker and Susan Leigh Star title the book's introduction with the phrase "To classify is human." They argue that our understanding of the world depends on the use and creation of implicit categories that serve to order the world. The difference between outdoors and indoors, for instance, dictates different styles of dress, types of activities, and so on.

But later on, Bowker and Star push a more incisive point about classification. "No one classification system organizes reality for everyone," they warn. "For example, the red light, yellow light, green light traffic light distinctions do not work for blind people (who need sound coding). In looking to classification schemes as ways of ordering the past, it is easy to forget those who have been overlooked in this way."[1]

Datasets are the end products of classification systems, the clean outputs of intentional orderings. My list of odd datasets was just the tiniest gesture at the many ways in which we have thought to classify our world.

"I'm always interested in the need for absence, what cannot be collected, what can't be contained, or what doesn't show up."—Mimi Ọnụọha

But the same way that a traffic light shows what we prioritize (vision) and cannot work for everyone (the blind), datasets point to their own contrasts—specifically the things that we haven't collected. And if it is true that we make sense of the world through exclusion, then perhaps there is a special type of meaning to be found in the things that we leave out. Here are examples of some of things we do not know:

- the number of people living off-lease in illegal housing situations in New York City
- gun trace data for people in the US who have bought guns
- which state people deported from the US were living in at the time of their removal
- the number of Rohingya people in Myanmar

"Missing datasets" is the term I use for these blank spots in a world that nowadays seems soaked in data. They form a ghostly parallel to the sheet of paper that occasionally adorns my desk. They, too, are the facts of our world, the vertices of measurements. But they are the ones that we know little about. Data are what people care about enough to measure. Missing datasets are the things that people care about but cannot measure.

My repository of missing datasets lives in forms far more permanent than a sheet of paper. One of these forms is an art piece called *The Library of Missing Datasets*. On first glance, it appears as simply a painted filing cabinet. But it holds within its drawers physical folders upon whose tabs the title of a missing dataset has been inscribed. The folders are empty. The content, like the data, is missing.

I've made myself a shepherd over this ever-growing library of missing datasets. Through them, I've learned that there are patterns to exclusion, structures that govern what

"Focusing on this moment of collection allows for space for the things that otherwise would be ignored or relegated to the sidelines or dismissed as complicating factors."—Mimi Onuoha

is and isn't able to be collected. I've taken note of the characteristics that make places immune to the growing datafication of the world. More than once I have found myself helping a group to collect some data that once was missing or justifying to another why not everything can or should be collected.

And as the list grows, I have increasingly been struck by the symbolic questions these shadow datasets raise. Their existence is assured: as long as we classify things and sort the world according to these classifications, there will always be missing datasets. There will always be bits that ooze out beneath spreadsheet cells, things that cannot be contained or that should not. Making sense of the world through exclusion implies a certain simplicity, and missing datasets, by virtue of their existence and nonexistence, challenge that simplicity.

I find this difficulty and its messiness thrilling, for it betrays a type of power. If something is always missing, it means that we always have the specter of a different kind of world, with different kinds of priorities. We do not collect data on police violence against Native Americans—but what kind of world would it be if we did?

These missing datasets do not provide answers, but the reminders they carry are poignant. We are the ones who render this world collectible. Each time we choose what data to collect and imbue that data with validity, we define the terms of the world. But if so, then we are also the ones capable of changing it and making it different, each and every time.

FIG 47. THE LIBRARY OF MISSING DATASETS. Artist and researcher Mimi Onuoha created this installation as "a physical repository of those things that have been excluded in a society where so much is collected." The installation draws our attention not to the data that has been collected, but the data that is missing, thereby revealing "our hidden social biases and indifferences."[2]

Anatomy of an AI System
Kate Crawford and Vladan Joler

A distinguished research professor at New York University and a senior principal researcher at MSR-NYC, Kate Crawford cofounded the AI Now Institute at NYU, the world's first university institute focused on researching the social implications of artificial intelligence (AI) and related technologies.

A professor of new media at the University of Novi Sad, Vladan Joler founded Share Foundation, an organization dedicated to protecting and implementing human rights standards in the digital environment.

Excerpt from "Anatomy of an AI System: The Amazon Echo As An Anatomical Map of Human Labor, Data and Planetary Resources," published by AI Now Institute and Share Lab, September 7, 2018.

XIX

In his one-paragraph short story "On Exactitude in Science," Jorge Luis Borges presents us with an imagined empire in which cartographic science became so developed and precise, that it needed a map on the same scale as the empire itself.

> In that Empire, the Art of Cartography attained such Perfection that the map of a single Province occupied the entirety of a City, and the map of the Empire, the entirety of a Province. In time, those Unconscionable Maps no longer satisfied, and the Cartographers Guilds struck a Map of the Empire whose size was that of the Empire, and which coincided point for point with it. The following Generations, who were not so fond of the Study of Cartography as their Forebears had been, saw that that vast map was Useless, and not without some Pitilessness was it, that they delivered it up to the Inclemencies of Sun and Winters. In the Deserts of the

West, still today, there are Tattered Ruins of that Map, inhabited by Animals and Beggars; in all the Land there is no other Relic of the Disciplines of Geography.[1]

Current machine-learning (ML) approaches are characterized by an aspiration to map the world, a full quantification of visual, auditory, and recognition regimes of reality. From the cosmological model for the universe to the world of human emotions as interpreted through the tiniest muscle movements in the human face, everything becomes an object of quantification. Jean-François Lyotard introduced the phrase "affinity to infinity" to describe how contemporary art, techno-science, and capitalism share the same aspiration to push boundaries toward a potentially infinite horizon.[2] The second half of the nineteenth century, with its focus on the construction of infrastructure and the uneven transition to industrialized society, generated enormous wealth for the small number of industrial magnates that monopolized exploitation of natural resources and production processes.

The new infinite horizon is data extraction, ML, and reorganizing information through AI systems of combined human and machinic processing. The territories are dominated by a few global mega-companies, which are creating new infrastructures and mechanisms for the accumulation of capital and exploitation of human and planetary resources.

Such unrestrained thirst for new resources and fields of cognitive exploitation has driven a search for ever deeper layers of data that can be used to quantify the human psyche, conscious and unconscious, private and public, idiosyncratic and general. In this way, we have seen the emergence of multiple cognitive economies from the attention economy, the surveillance economy, the reputation economy, and the emotion economy, as well as the quantification and commodification of trust and evidence through cryptocurrencies.[3]

Increasingly, the process of quantification is reaching into the human affective, cognitive, and physical worlds. Training sets exist for emotion detection, for family resemblance, for tracking an individual as they age, and for human actions like sitting down, waving, raising a glass, or crying. Every form of biodata—including forensic, biometric, sociometric, and psychometric—are being captured and logged into databases for AI training. That quantification often runs on very limited foundations: datasets like AVA (Atomic Visual Actions), which primarily shows women in the "playing with children" action category and men in the "kicking a person" category. The training sets for AI systems claim to be reaching into the fine-grained nature of everyday life, but they repeat the most stereotypical and restricted social patterns, reinscribing a normative vision of the human past and projecting it into the human future.

XX

....

The new gold rush in the context of artificial intelligence is to enclose different fields of human knowing, feeling, and action in order to capture and privatize those fields. When in November 2015, DeepMind Technologies Ltd. got access to the health records of 1.6 million identifiable patients of the Royal Free Hospital, we witnessed a particular form of privatization: the extraction of knowledge value.[4] A dataset may still be publicly owned, but the metavalue of the data—the model created by it—is privately owned. While there are many good reasons to seek to improve public health, there is a real risk if it comes at the cost of a stealth privatization of public medical services. That is a future where expert local human labor in the public system is augmented and sometimes replaced with centralized, privately owned corporate AI systems that are using public data to generate enormous wealth for the very few.

XXI

At this moment in the twenty-first century, we see a new form of extractivism that is well underway: one that reaches into the furthest corners of the biosphere and the deepest layers of human cognitive and affective being. Many of

"Put simply: each small moment of convenience—be it answering a question, turning on a light, or playing a song—requires a vast planetary network, fueled by the extraction of non-renewable materials, labor, and data."—Kate Crawford and Vladan Joler

the assumptions about human life made by ML systems are narrow, normative, and laden with error. Yet they are inscribing and building those assumptions into a new world and will increasingly play a role in how opportunities, wealth, and knowledge are distributed.

The stack that is required to interact with an Amazon Echo goes well beyond the multilayered "technical stack" of data modeling, hardware, servers, and networks. The full stack reaches much further into capital, labor, and nature, and demands an enormous amount of each. The true costs of these systems—social, environmental, economic, and political—remain hidden and may stay that way for some time.

We offer up this map and essay as a way to begin seeing across a wider range of system extractions. The scale required to build artificial intelligence systems is too complex, too obscured by intellectual property law, and too mired in logistical complexity to fully comprehend in the moment. Yet you draw on it every time you issue a simple voice command to a small cylinder in your living room: "Alexa, what time is it?"

And so the cycle continues.

FIG 48. ANATOMY OF AN AI SYSTEM (following spread)
According to researchers Kate Crawford and Vladan Joler of the AI Now Institute, this project—a detailed infographic and essay—"depicts the actual infrastructure required to deliver the result of users' operation of smart devices, from human labor, extraction and refining of rare earths, cable networks, server farms and satellite systems to data flows." The infographic (a portion of which is shown on the following spread) raises questions around the heavy touch points between AI and material resources, despite the seamless experience through which users interact with the technology.[5]

Anatomy of an AI system

An anatomical case study of the Amazon echo as a artificial intelligence system made of human labor

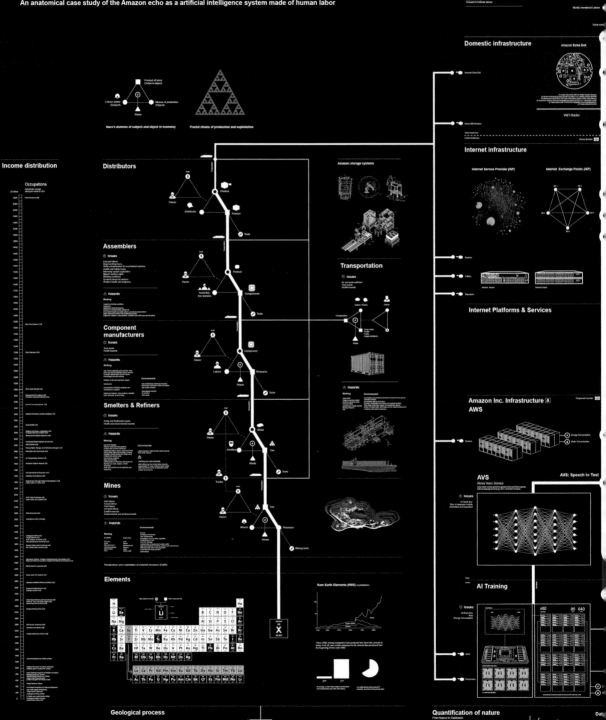

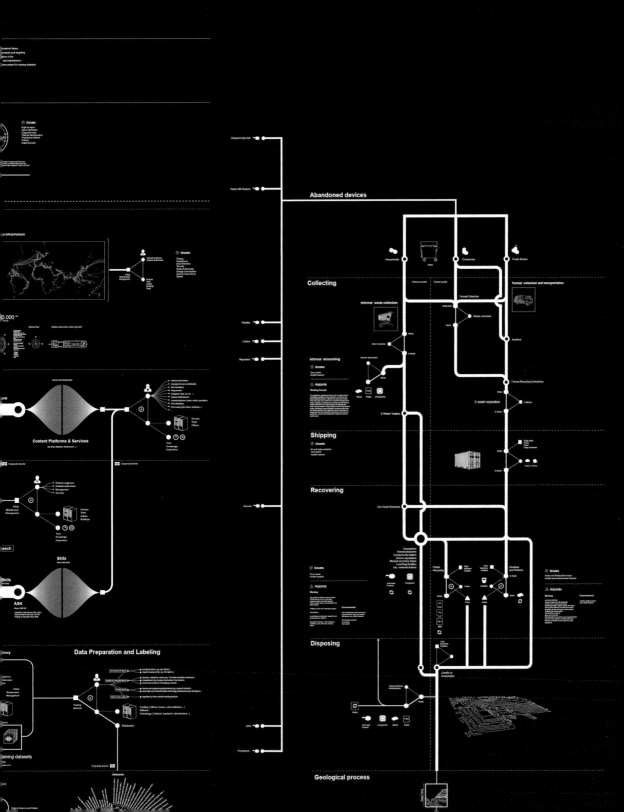

CHAPTER FOUR

Who's Afraid
of Machine
Learning?

Who's afraid of a little machine learning (ML)? To understand this technology, designers need to get into the weeds—just a little. There are three main types of machine-learning algorithms: supervised learning, unsupervised learning, and reinforcement learning. Let's start with supervised learning.

SUPERVISED LEARNING

Supervised learning relies upon a full set of labeled data. (Labeled data means data that has been tagged, effectively placing the data into categories. Think spreadsheets of information.) Algorithms examine this labeled data, learn from patterns in the data, and then make predictions. It's the most prevalent form of machine learning today; therefore, it's worth examining closely.

Researchers would choose supervised learning to take on problems of *classification* or problems of *regression*. If we want the algorithms to predict the discrete category or "class" that new data will fall within, we would use classification. If we want the algorithms to predict outputs related to a real-valued number, we would use *regression*.

If you are feeling overwhelmed with technical jargon right now, bear with me. I'll explain each of these.

CORN SNAKE OR COPPERHEAD?
IF IT'S IN YOUR YARD, YOU NEED TO KNOW.

Let's start with a supervised learning strategy that uses classification. Imagine that snakes begin to infest your neighborhood. Neighbors begin posting pictures online to determine whether the particular snake in their own yard is a copperhead—poisonous—or the similar-looking corn snake—harmless. Their kids play outside, and they need to know. You decide to design an app to solve this problem. To develop the app, you need a system for differentiating snake species.

First, you gather training data: a set of snakes individually labeled as either a copperhead or a corn snake. This data composes our "ground truth." We can also refer to these two labels as classes.

Next, we need to determine features that the system can use to distinguish one class from the other. In this example, let's identify two features: length and mass. (Note that this is only for the sake of our example. Do not actually use these features to classify snakes and risk the life of a kid.)

A data scientist, developer, or designer might determine these specific features, or a team of experts in a particular domain might select the features and label the data. This is called annotation. In our example, we might bring in a team of expert herpetologists. The herpetologists would create a document with a set of rules for annotation. This process can be straightforward, but it can also be quite controversial. Participants might disagree over which features to use or what dataset is most appropriate. Domain-specific experts

LABELED DATA

SNAKE	LENGTH	MASS
Copperhead	11.7	3.4
Copperhead	10.2	4.4
Corn Snake	12.8	5.0
Copperhead	12.0	3.0
Corn Snake	12.4	4.8
Corn Snake	11.9	4.5

might also be worried about sharing confidential knowledge about the data with the data science team running the ML algorithms.

Let's assume that our process goes smoothly. Once the features are selected, we clean the resulting labeled data, ridding it of errors, inconsistencies, missing data, and duplicates. We then randomize the order of the data and look for bias in the training examples. If there are too many copperheads used in the training data, more copperheads will subsequently be identified in the system, biasing it toward copperheads. We've seen this play out in numerous real-world examples when, for instance, an ML system has been trained using too many examples of one skin tone and not enough of others.[1]

We then set aside a portion of the data to use to evaluate our system later.

Now the fun begins. We choose a learning algorithm and instruct that algorithm to build a model from the training set. In this example, we need to teach the system to separate the data into two different categories—or classes—of snake species so utilizing a classification model makes sense.

Note that this approach, like all ML, builds a statistical model. We can't achieve 100 percent accuracy with any model, but we will work to select and tweak our model to be as accurate as possible. ML, like design, is iterative. To increase the predictive power, we will need to refine the model throughout the process.

There are multiple strategies that a classification model could employ to achieve our goal, such as Decision Tree, K-Nearest Neighbor, and Naive Bayes. In this instance, let's select a Decision Tree strategy. When we run this selected strategy, the learning algorithms will, in essence, create a model that draws a line through the data creating a boundary separation. Based upon their features, some of the snakes will fall under the class of copperhead and some will fall under the class of corn snake. The algorithms will then check the results against the training data for accuracy and redraw the line

STATISTICAL MODEL: a mathematical representation of data based on relationships observed within the data

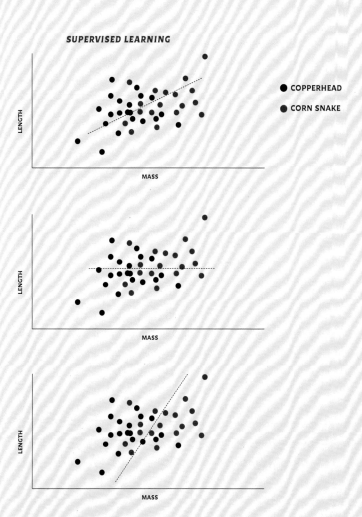

SUPERVISED LEARNING

- ● COPPERHEAD
- ● CORN SNAKE

repeatedly to find the optimal boundary separation—the position in which the most snakes are accurately classified under their respective snake species.

Humans oversee this process, working to improve the results. As noted previously, the training data matters. We may need to add or delete training examples, particularly outliers, to increase accuracy. Or we may need to adjust the features. We may even try a different classification strategy, like K-Nearest-Neighbor or Naive Bayes. Each strategy will have its own advantages and trade-offs.

OUTLIERS: atypical values within a dataset; values that lie outside the distribution pattern

When we feel confident about the results, we can run the model on the labeled data that we set aside earlier for the evaluation phase. Depending on the results, we can keep working on the model or accept the accuracy rate.

Eventually, we should be able to run any copperhead or corn snake through this system and identify its species at a high rate of accuracy, not 100 percent but a high rate. We call the computer's decision that a certain snake is a copperhead or corn snake a prediction.

Let's step back and appreciate the beauty of the resulting system. We no longer need human judgment to determine the species of snake. And we don't need to program manual rules. In addition, if we have built-in feedback, the algorithms can learn from each misclassification and continually improve the results once the system is in play. Phew, the kids—and the corn snakes—are safe!

In this example we used two classes—copperhead and corn snake—and two features—mass and length. Keep in mind that predictive algorithms can use many, many classes and hundreds if not thousands of features.

REGRESSION

Regression differs from classification because it allows us to explore values—and thus make predictions—in between and beyond discrete classes. Regression can do this because the output is numerical (or continuous). We wouldn't pick a regression model for classifying snakes because, in our example, we want each snake to be identified as either one species or another.

We would use regression in situations in which we want the system to identify values in between or beyond what we initially defined in the training data. Such values might include the future price of something, customer-satisfaction level, or the grades of a student. In each of these instances, the algorithms would use the relationship between the continuous number and some other variable(s) to make predictions.

We used a classification strategy to organize input data (our snakes) into discrete classes. Using regression, we want the algorithms to predict a specific numerical value rather than a class. Models commonly used in regression include linear models, polynomial regression models, and, for more complex regression problems, neural networks.

For example, we might use regression to predict the future price of a house depending upon the rate of local job growth, or the level of customer satisfaction depending upon wait time, or the grade of a student in relation to the hours spent working in a studio.

Let's envision the process of running a model to predict a student's grade (a numerical value between 0 and 100). First we would label training examples of student grades, the dependent variable, paired with an independent variable, such as the amount of time physically spent weekly in the studio. Once we established some labeled examples, we could train the ML algorithms to predict the future grade of any student based on the independent variable—the amount of studio time. Now, think bigger. Just as with classification, predictive algorithms could compute a problem much more complex than our simple example. Instead of one variable, in this case time spent in the studio, there could be many.

Note that even though with regression the algorithms can make value predictions beyond those explicitly expressed in the training data (i.e., we don't have to provide examples of every possible grade/hour combination), they are doing so based on labeled data and defined variables. When we get to unsupervised learning, this will change.

DEPENDENT VARIABLE: a variable whose value depends on that of another

INDEPENDENT VARIABLE: the input for a process that is being analyzed (i.e., the feature)

SUPERVISED LEARNING: KEY TAKEAWAYS
- requires labeled training data
- has a clearly defined goal: "Computer, look for these particular patterns in the data so that you might predict x."
- the most prevalent form of ML today

UNSUPERVISED LEARNING

In unsupervised learning, an expert does not label the training data or provide the features/variables. Instead, the algorithms parse through input data looking for regularities or patterns that have not been prespecified. So, for example, instead of feeding our algorithms lots of images of snakes, already labeled as corn snake or copperhead, we might just give the system lots of snake images of both species and ask the algorithms to look for patterns to differentiate between the two. The algorithms themselves would then identify variables to reveal patterns. We wouldn't necessarily know how the algorithms selected the variables—and there could be thousands. We could even ask the algorithms to look for interesting patterns with less of a prescribed goal in mind.

Supervised learning requires a supervisor—someone to label the data. Unsupervised learning doesn't. Bypassing the supervisor can result in striking, unexpected outcomes.

When might humans use unsupervised learning? We might select unsupervised learning in situations in which the outcome is unclear or the analysis process too complex for a human to determine key differentiating labels and variables. Such complex situations might include identifying a human face, fraud detection, or predicting consumer behavior. Unsupervised learning also plays a key role in deep learning— to be discussed later.

When ML algorithms detect complex patterns using thousands of variables, humans sometimes struggle to understand how the machines arrived at their predictions. We call this the Black Box Problem. This might not be a big deal when a targeted ad miscalculates our interests. However, if we were denied parole based on a machine prediction of recidivism, it would suddenly be a huge deal—particularly if no one could explain how the decision was made.[2]

In addition to successfully analyzing highly complex situations, unsupervised learning algorithms can cut down on the time and expense necessitated by labeled data. Remember that supervised learning algorithms require labeled data and identified features for training. Cheaper, more easily acquired, unlabeled data can be fed into unsupervised learning algorithms. All that unstructured, multimodal data—images, sounds, movement—referenced earlier becomes rich fodder for these systems.[3]

Common strategies in unsupervised learning include clustering and dimensionality reduction. Let's look at clustering.

CLUSTERING

Using this strategy, algorithms compute clusters or groups within the input data, i.e., data points with similar features are grouped together and data points with dissimilar features apart. Popular clustering algorithms include K-Means, Mean Shift, DBSCAN, Expectation-Maximation Clustering using Gaussian Mixture Models, and Agglomerative Hierarchical Clustering.

A retail company might use clustering to segment their customers. They could provide existing customer data points as input—age, zip code, gender, purchase history, etc.—and then run clustering algorithms to establish new groupings. The algorithms might discover customer segments that a designer or marketer would not typically envision. Or the model might reveal outliers that could inspire niche markets.[4] We could

UNSUPERVISED LEARNING: CLUSTERING

also use clustering to identify future trends like the professional turnover rate in a particular industry.[5] Darktrace, a cybersecurity company, uses unsupervised learning to learn patterns of normal behavior in a system, and then looks for anomalies—suspicious behavior—that could be cyberattacks. Rather than rely upon labeled data built from accumulated knowledge of past security threats, the system can look for threats that companies haven't yet identified.[6] Clustering can reveal unexpected insights that push beyond the typical human perspective.

157 | Who's Afraid of Machine Learning?

UNSUPERVISED LEARNING: KEY TAKEAWAYS
- can detect patterns in situations too complex for human analysis
- does not require labeled data and/or identified features/variables
- can arrive at unexpected insights

REINFORCEMENT LEARNING
In both supervised and unsupervised learning, algorithms make predictions based on training data. We can think of this as historical data because it already exists in the world. Knowledge of the past dictates predictions of the future. We talked about some of the negative implications of this in chapter three. Here, let's just consider the following, "Would you want to always be judged by your past behavior?"

In contrast, reinforcement learning algorithms do not make predictions based on historical data. Instead, these algorithms build a prediction model on the fly by interacting with an environment using trial and error. Here's how it works: an agent tries out possible actions within an environment. Each interaction with the environment produces insight— which acts as the input data. The agent then uses this data to iteratively adjust their actions to achieve a specific goal— a reward.

AGENT: the one that decides what action to take in response to rewards or punishments

ENVIRONMENT: the surroundings or conditions within which an agent takes action

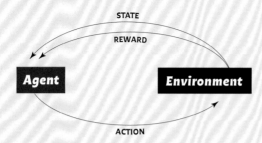

COMPONENTS OF REINFORCEMENT LEARNING

STATE

REWARD

Agent

Environment

ACTION

Think of a video game as an easy analogy for reinforcement learning. In such a game, players move through the game environment. By "playing," or interacting within that environment, they learn which actions move them toward the goal of winning and which do not. They repeat actions that work, using the resulting insight to inform subsequent behavior.

This form of ML is most akin to the way we humans might acquire knowledge. To learn to roller skate, we put on skates and try. Each time we fall, we learn something about staying upright. We achieve our goal—moving around on skates while maintaining our balance—by putting this new knowledge into action.

In 2017, DeepMind employed reinforcement learning combined with deep convolutional networks, using a program called AlphaGo, to beat a human champion at the nuanced game of Go. Later the same year, they released a more advanced program called AlphaZero that mastered chess, shogi, and Go. According to DeepMind, the style and complexity of each game determined the training time: nine hours for chess, twelve hours for shogi, and thirteen days for Go.[7] Compare this to the years of intensive training that mastery requires of a human. Now imagine this technology applied to larger high-impact problems that require strategic action—global warming, for instance. Prior to this moment in 2017, according to Pedro Domingos, author of *The Master Algorithm*, "The supervised-learning people would make fun of the reinforcement-learning people."[8] DeepMind set everyone straight.

DEEP CONVOLUTIONAL NETWORK: a specific kind of deep neural network that has a convolution layer

Because reinforcement learning algorithms can interact with an unpredictable digital or physical environment, we often see them employed in gaming AIs, logistics, resource management, robotics, and autonomous car navigation systems. Researchers can conveniently run these algorithms through millions of virtual simulations before taking their products into the world.[9] Computer scientist Mark Crowley, of the University of Waterloo, currently trains virtual fires, using reinforcement learning so that he might predict the path of future wildfires.[10] Uber refines their self-driving AI platform by putting it through thousands of virtual simulations, using predictive algorithms to play the self-driving AI against an equally intelligent environment.[11] The training period of these algorithms can be lengthy—typically longer than that of supervised learning systems despite the breakneck speed of AlphaZero—but the ability to respond to environments *in real time* can trump that substantial training time.[12]

Common reinforcement learning strategies include Deep Deterministic Policy Gradient, Q-Learning, State-Action-Reward-State-Action, and Deep Q-Networks. Note that in each of these strategies, as in unsupervised learning, no supervisor oversees the process. Because there is no supervisor, the supervisor cannot introduce bias into the system. To be clear, this does not eliminate all possibilities for bias, but it does get rid of one common avenue.[13] This lack of a supervisor also means that reinforcement learning can introduce alien strategies for "winning," i.e., achieving the reward, and then, in turn, teach these unusual strategies back to humans. In the previous example of AlphaGo and AlphaZero, Go champions studied the winning strategies employed by these programs and copied the tactics in their own subsequent games. Some of the tactics, however, were unusable because, try as they might, human players found them incomprehensible.[14] With less overt bias and the introduction of mind-boggling new strategies, reinforcement learning is pulling in big research dollars right now.[15]

REINFORCEMENT LEARNING: KEY TAKEAWAYS
· gains insight through trial and error
· model interacts with an environment
  sequentially over time
· eliminates supervisor bias
· can introduce alien approaches that prove
  useful to humans

CONCLUSION

Although we considered each ML category separately, many researchers mix these categories together in practice. Semi-supervised learning refers specifically to blends of supervised and unsupervised learning, but researchers can also use all three categories to achieve their goals.[16] This process can be messy and complex, requiring a deep knowledge of mathematics and statistics and a big helping of intuition. Training a set of algorithms requires a different skill set than programming explicit logic-based instructions.

SEMI-SUPERVISED LEARNING: a training approach in machine learning that combines supervised and unsupervised methods

This shift from programming to training produces a relationship with machines that is less clear cut and more difficult to control. Jason Tanz, the site director of *Wired*, explains, "If in the old view programmers were like gods, authoring the laws that govern computer systems, now they're like parents or dog trainers. And as any parent or dog owner can tell you, that is a much more mysterious relationship to find yourself in."[17] Designers thrive in this kind of liminal space. Working with data scientists, we can begin prototyping user experience and interface possibilities that map out such emerging relationships between human and machine.

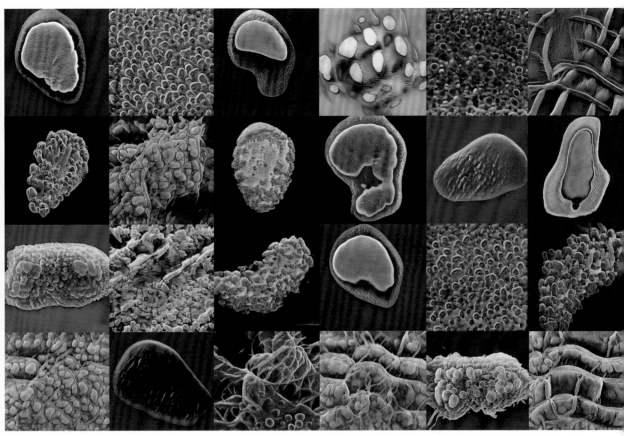

FIG 49. MICROBIAL COSMOLOGIES. Designer Anastasiia Raina used StyleGAN2 to generate "a set of artificial microorganisms that are yet to be discovered." After training deep learning algorithms on thousands of images of microorganisms, she extrapolated images in latent space—a typology of all AI-generated images which spans over 512 dimensions. As Raina explains, "This is a vast space for image variation, producing an infinite number of mutations."[18] Such work exemplifies the complex morphologies possible for designers to explore in an ML world.

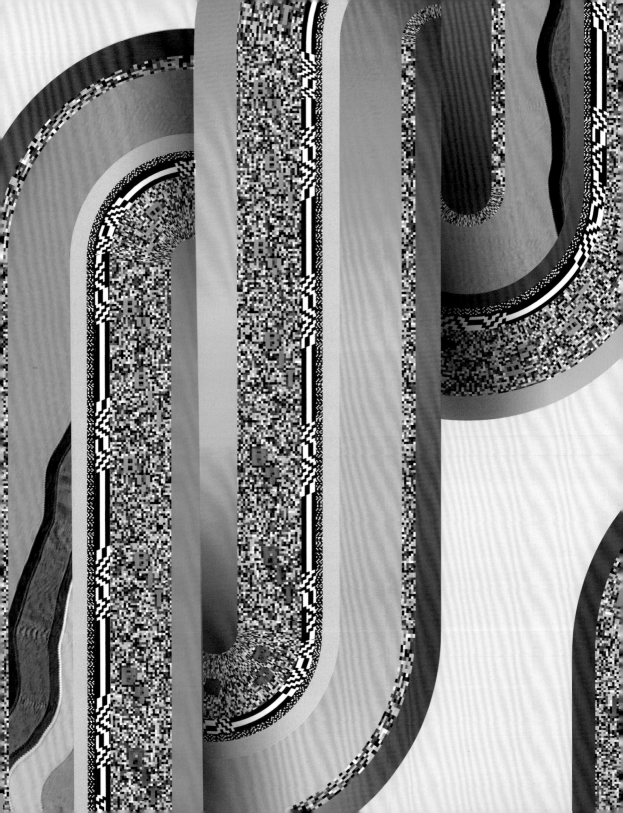

The Future: Exciting but Fraught

For the breadth of this book we have grappled with how machine learning (ML) impacts what we create as designers. Let's now briefly consider ways ML might affect *how* we will design in the coming years. Not only will the interface/products that we create exhibit intelligence, but also will our creative tools.

In chapter two, we discussed how ML has changed the way humans relate to machines by enabling them to communicate with tech via language, gesture, movement, emotion, etc. These same capabilities will enable designers to engage with creative tools in more intuitive ways, supplanting the mouse, trackpad, and touchscreen. Simply asking software to perform an action—rather than clicking and dragging through a menu to find the right tool—will, for example, allow designers to bypass hours of busywork, not to mention perusing dense tutorials.[1] Perhaps the very concept of a "tool" will grow irrelevant. The more natural and personalized the interaction, the more creative software might feel like an extension of ourselves—and our individual creative approaches—rather than a separate clunky software package.

ESCAPE THE CUBICLE

If design tools combine relational interaction with artificial intelligence's (AI) growing awareness of context, designers could, at long last, escape desk and screen. We could design for the world as we stand in the world, creating while situated in augmented physical space. Silka Sietsma asserts, "We're at the event horizon of a new era of *spatial computing*—a world where digital experiences mesh with physical reality. Immersive, 3D technologies like AR (augmented reality) and VR (virtual reality), along with voice and embedded sensors, are all converging into a new medium, powered by artificial intelligence."[2] It is within this new medium—this confluence of physical and digital, that our future design practice will evolve.

How else will ML impact design practice? Patrick Hebron suggests that we consider the future in terms of "scaffolding complexity." While reflecting on CAD systems and the future of creative tools, he points out: "These tools make it possible to conceive of systems that are too grand and complex for any one individual to keep all of their big picture goals and specific details in mind simultaneously." Hebron also notes, "The Florence Cathedral took about one hundred and forty years to go from initial conception to project completion. A much more complicated and recent building, the Burj Khalifa, took about five years." Our tasks and aesthetic goals, he asserts, will continue to evolve as ML enables us to enter terrain that we could not even envision without AI. "Machine intelligence," he explains, "will enable creatives to do even more and to think even bigger."[3]

RETURN OF THE CENTAUR

In such a vision, humans and intelligent machines work together to arrive at solutions unattainable by either alone. Remember the concept of the centaur? Rather than automating away the designer, designers join forces with AI, augmenting their abilities with ML—a fusing of intelligences. Matt Jones of Google AI argues that to truly take advantage of AI, we must accept its alien nature.[4]

Alternative models of "intelligence" exist already in the natural world—specialized forms of cognition distributed across organisms, nerve cells, and root-fungi networks rather centralized in a single human brain. Myriad recent books have raised popular awareness of these alternatives, such as Peter Godfrey-Smith's book, *Other Minds: The Octopus, the Sea, and the Deep Origins of Consciousness* and Peter Wohlleben's treatise, *The Hidden Life of Trees.*[5] As posited by posthuman theorists like N. Katherine Hayles and Donna Haraway, we should expand our understanding to other forms of cognition as we coevolve with our tools. In essence, we must recognize that integrating ML into design practice will not feel like adding a supersmart fake human to our creative team but, instead, will be something else entirely. Like bacteria, trees, or earthworms, AI will think differently than we do.

THE COMBO, PLEASE

Since the 1960s, we have imagined that AI will take over form-making, serving up a multitude of form variations from which a designer can simply choose—a fast forwarding of the design process.[6] But, it turns out, the most powerful application of ML is not speeding up our process to arrive at the same kind of conclusions. The most powerful applications combine machine intelligence with human intelligence to take us along new paths entirely.

Janelle Shane puts it simply: "Working with AI is a lot less like working with another human and a lot more like working with some kind of weird force of nature."[7] This force of nature will tirelessly work toward exactly the goal that we give it, so we have to figure out the right goal. And we shouldn't expect it—or want it—to solve the problem like a human. Shane points to a project by David Ha, a researcher at Google Brain, in which Ha asked an AI to assemble some parts into a robot to move from Point A to Point B. Rather than solving the problem by assembling a nimble robot, as Ha intended, the AI combined the parts into a tower that could just fall over and land on Point B.[8] As Hebron comments, "The world is full of human thinkers. And if we want human thinking, we should probably go to humans for it. There are a lot of them."[9] If we don't waste time trying to force AI to think like a human, we can arrive at Point B—and Points C, D, and E—in fresh, alien ways.

Novel AI strategies, however, mean little without perspective and purpose. Humans do need to be part of the equation. Remember the human-AI chess teams that triumphed over solo humans or solo AI competitors? The confluence of human *and* machine is key. As Shane explains, "The AI has no understanding of the consequences."[10] Humans bring that understanding to the equation. We human designers must be there to frame the right problems—the problems that will move us toward future points that truly benefit humanity.

FINAL THOUGHTS

We've come far together in the pages of this book. The future is…fraught. Our profession stands on the cusp. Designers must strive to understand ML capabilities, so that we can engage with it as a design material and a creative force. If we do not, we will fall victim to it. We will create within the parameters that the technology sets for us, rather than the other way around.

Through ML we have amazing potential to provide emotional insight to those on the autism spectrum, to reduce gender and racial bias in hiring and lending practices, to springboard creatives into unexpected, wicked problem-solving spaces. However, we can also do the exact opposite—exploit the vulnerable, bias the future by relying upon the past, replace humans by automating away skills that we want and need to maintain autonomy and agency, relegate essential choices to a technology that has no understanding of human consequence.

Questions around AI and humanity have been hotly debated since at least the middle of the twentieth century. As design professor and historian Molly Wright Steenson points out, "If we understand that we've been asking these questions for a long time, we might have better expectations about how hard it is to find answers."[11] These are complex questions with wide implications.

The terrain is tricky. The future is uncertain. Exciting? Yes. Terrifying? Yes. We have many critical choices ahead. Let's take on those choices together, thoughtfully, one design at a time.

Notes

CHAPTER ONE: PEEK INSIDE THE BLACK BOX

1. Amir Gandomi and Murtaza Haider, "Beyond the Hype: Big Data Concepts, Methods, and Analytics," *International Journal of Information Management* 35, no. 2 (2015): 137.

2. Sentient, a digital military brain, exemplifies this on a large scale. See Sarah Scoles, "It's Sentient: Meet the Classified Artificial Brain Being Developed by US Intelligence Programs," *The Verge*, July 31, 2019, https://www.theverge.com/2019/7/31/20746926/ sentient-national-reconnaissance-office-spy-satellites-artificial-intelligence-ai.

3. Note that current research is exploring how to effectively use smaller datasets. George Lawton, "Using Small Datasets for Machine Learning Models Sees Growth," SearchEnterpriseAI.com, Nov 13, 2019, https://searchenterpriseai.techtarget.com/feature/Using-small-data-sets-for-machine-learning-models-sees-growth.

4. John Seabrook, "The Next Word: Where Will Predictive Text Take Us?," *The New Yorker*, October 14, 2019, https://www.newyorker.com/magazine/2019/10/14/can-a-machine-learn-to-write-for-the-new-yorker.

5. Ajay Agrawal, Joshua Gans, and Avi Goldfarb, *Prediction Machines the Simple Economics of Artificial Intelligence* (Boston, MA: Harvard Business Review Press, 2018).

6. Patrick Hebron, *Machine Learning for Designers* (Sebastopol, CA: O'Reilly, 2016).

7. Jason Tanz, "Soon We Won't Program Computers. We'll Train Them Like Dogs," *Wired*, May 17, 2016, https://www.wired.com/2016/05/the-end-of-code/.

8. Ryszard Michalski, "Pattern Recognition as Rule-Guided Inductive Inference," *IEEE Transactions on Pattern Analysis and Machine Intelligence* PAMI-2, no. 4 (July 1980): 349–61, https://doi.org/10.1109/TPAMI.1980.4767034.

9. Mimi Onuoha and Mother Cyborg, *A People's Guide to AI* (Detroit, MI: Allied Media, 2018).

10. William D. Nordhaus, "Do Real-Output and Real-Wage Measures Capture Reality? The History of Lighting Suggests Not," in *The Economics of New Goods*, ed. Timothy F. Bresnahan and Robert J. Gordon (Chicago: University of Chicago Press, 1996), 27–70; see also Kevin Kelly, *The Inevitable: Understanding the 12 Technological Forces That Will Shape Our Future* (London: Penguin, 2017).

11. Agrawal, Gan, and Goldfarb, *Prediction Machines*, 11.

12. Ibid. 12.

13. Joël van Bodegraven, "How Anticipatory Design Will Challenge Our Relationship with Technology," in *The AAAI 2017 Spring Symposium on Designing the User Experience of Machine Learning Systems Technical Report SS-17-04* (Palo Alto, CA: AAI, 2017), 436.

14. Aaron Weyenberg, "The Ethics of Good Design: A Principle for the Connected Age," *Medium.com*, November 20, 2016, https://medium.com/swlh/dieter-rams-ten-principles-for-good-design-the-1st-amendment-4e73111a18e4.

15. Ibid.

16. Seabrook, "The Next Word."

17. Elizabeth B.-N. Sanders, "From User-Centered to Participatory Design Approaches," in *Design and the Social Sciences: Making Connections*, ed. Jorge Frascara (London: Taylor & Francis, 2002).

18. Tanmay Bakshi, "Technology That Tackles the Teen Suicide Epidemic" (filmed December 2017 in San Francisco, California. TED@IBM video, 9:24), https://www.ted.com/ talks/tanmay_bakshi_technology_that_tackles_the_ teen_suicide_epidemic.

19. Qian Yang, John Zimmerman, Aaron Steinfeld, Lisa Carey, and James F. Antaki, "Investigating the Heart Pump Implant Decision Process: Opportunities for Decision Support Tools to Help." In *Proceedings of the 2016 CHI Conference on Human Factors in Computing Systems* (CHI '16). Association for Computing Machinery, New York, NY, USA, 4477–4488. DOI: https://doi. org/10.1145/2858036.2858373. 20.

20. Kevin Rowe, "How Search Engines Use Machine Learning: 9 Things We Know for Sure," *Search Engine Journal*, February 23, 2018, https://www.search-enginejournal.com/how-search-engines-use-machine-learning/224451/#close.

21. The research team includes John Bass, Mike Kowolenko, and Van Daughtry.

22. Lana Bandoim, "How McDonald's Plans To Use Machine Learning To Personalize The Drive-Thru," *Forbes*, April 30, 2019, https://www.forbes.com/sites/lanabandoim/2019/04/30/how-mcdonalds-plans-to-use-machine-learning-to-personalize-the-drive-thru; see also PSFK, "Taco Bell Leverages AI to Personalize Digital Menus for App Members," *PSFK*, Oct 2, 2020, https://www.psfk.com/2020/10/taco-bell-ai-personalized-menus.html.

23. Eli Pariser, "Beware Online 'Filter Bubbles,'" (filmed March 2011 in Long Beach, California. TED video, 8:49), https://www.ted.com/talks/eli_pariser_beware_online_filter_bubbles.

24. Douglas Rushkoff, *Team Human* (New York: Norton, 2019); Geert Lovink, *Sad By Design: On Platform Nihilism* (London: Pluto Press, 2019); Shoshana Zuboff, *The Age of Surveillance Capitalism: the Fight for Human Future at the New Frontier of Power* (New York: PublicAffairs, 2019); Yuval Noah Harari, *21 Lessons for the 21st Century* (New York: Spiegel & Grau, 2018).

25. See MIT's Council on Extended Intelligence, https://globalcxi.org/. Research efforts include a Wellbeing Indicator template for governments and organizations to utilize in helping society redefine and reprioritize genuine metrics of prosperity.

26. Aaron Shapiro coined "Anticipatory Design." See "The Next Big Thing In Design? Less Choice," *Fast Company*, April 15, 2015, https://www. fastcodesign.com/3045039/the-next-big-thing-in-design-fewer-choices.

27. Agrawal, Gan, and Goldfarb, *Prediction Machines*, 17.

28. Nenad Tomašev, et al., "A Clinically Applicable Approach to Continuous Prediction of Future Acute Kidney Injury," *Nature* 572, (2019), 116–19. https://doi.org/10.1038/s41586-019-1390-1.

29. Jeffrey De Fauw et al., "Clinically Applicable Deep Learning for Diagnosis and Referral in Retinal Disease," *Nature Medicine* 24 (August 2018), https://doi.org/10.1038/s41591-018-0107-6.

30. David Rose, *Enchanted Objects: Design, Human Desire, and The Internet of Things* (New York: Scribner, 2014).

31. Shapiro, "The Next Big Thing," 32.

32. van Bodegraven, "How Anticipatory Design Will Challenge."

33. Graham Dove, Kim Halskow, Jodi Forlizzi, John Zimmerman, "UX Design Innovation: Challenges for Working with Machine Learning as a Design Material," in *Proceedings of the 2017 CHI Conference on Human Factors in Computing Systems*, ed. Gloria Mark (Denver, CO: CHI: 2017): 280.

34. Mike Kuniavsky, "The User Experience of Predictive Behavior in the (Consumer) Internet of Things," (presentation, *RE.WORK Connect Summit*, San Francisco, November 6, 2015).

35. Qian Yang, "The Role of Design in Creating Machine-Learning-Enhanced User Experience," in *The AAAI 2017 Spring Symposium on Designing the User Experience of Machine Learning Systems Technical Report SS-17-04* (Palo Alto, CA: AAAI, 2017), 206.

36. Betti Marenko and Philip van Allen, "Animistic Design: How to Reimagine Digital Interaction between the Human and the Nonhuman," *Digital Creativity* 27, no. 1 (2016): 52–70.

37. Philip van Allen, personal interview with author, May 6, 2020

38. Marenko and van Allen, "Animistic Design."

39. Ibid. van Allen.

40. Janelle Shane, *You Look Like a Thing and I Love You* (New York: Little, Brown, 2019).

41. John Zimmerman, personal interview with author, February 4, 2020.

42. Yang, Qian & Scuito, Alex & Zimmerman, John & Forlizzi, Jodi & Steinfeld, Aaron, "Investigating How Experienced UX Designers Effectively Work with Machine Learning," in *Proceedings of the 2018 Designing Interactive Systems Conference*, (Hong Kong: 2018). 10.1145/3196709.3196730.

43. The term "Design Material" references the work of Donald Schön, a philosopher who presented an influential approach to cognitive design theory in the 1980s. He considered design as a "reflective activity." We see this play out through Schön's core concept of "reflection-in-action" in which "doing and thinking are complementary. Doing extends thinking in the tests, moves, and probes of experimental action, and reflection feeds on doing and its results. Each feeds the other, and each sets boundaries for the other." In Schön's epistemology of professional design practice, designers converse with design situations through the process of making. Design manifests through a "reflective conversation with the materials of a design situation." See Donald Schön, *The Reflective Practitioner: How Professionals Think in Action* (New York: Basic Books, 1984).

44. John Zimmerman, personal interview with author, February 4, 2020.

45. Ibid.

46. Ibid.

47. van Allen, interview.

48. Philip van Allen, "Delft AI Toolkit: A Tool for the Design of AI," philvanallen.com, https://www.philvanallen.com/portfolio/delft-ai-toolkit/.

49. Rebecca Fiebrink, "Creative Coding Symposium at Electric," *Creative Coding Symposium at Electric*, (Queensgate, UK: 2019), https://www.youtube.com/watch?v=Qo6n8MuEgdQ.

50. Fiebrink, "Creative Coding Symposium."

51. Andreas Refsgaard, "Playful Machine Learning" (presentation, *Design Matters Conference '19*, Copenhagen, September 18, 2019).

PHILIP VAN ALLEN, "ANIMISTIC DESIGN"

1. Philip van Allen, personal interview with author, May 6, 2020.

ANASTASIIA RAINA, "MACHINES HAVE EYES"

1. Sean B. Carroll, *Endless Forms Most Beautiful: The New Science of Evo Devo and the Making of the Animal Kingdom* (New York: Norton, 2005).

2. Derek E. Moulton, et al., "Multiscale Integration of Environmental Stimuli in Plant Tropism Produces Complex Behaviors," *BioRxiv*, Cold Spring Harbor Laboratory, Jan 1, 2020, www.biorxiv.org/content/10.1101/2020.07.30.228973v1.

3. Kelly A. McLaughlin and Michael Levin, "Bioelectric Signaling in Regeneration: Mechanisms of Ionic Controls of Growth and Form," *Developmental Biology* 433, no.2 (2018): 177–89.

CHAPTER TWO: SEIZE THE DATA

1. Adam Cutler, "Can We Be Friends with Our AI?" Filmed December 2017 in San Francisco, California. TED@IBM video, https://www.ted.com/talks/adam_cutler_can_we_be_friends_with_our_ai

2. Silka Sietsma. Interview with Helen Armstrong. Personal interview. May 29, 2020.

3. Paul Pangaro "Conversation is More Than Interaction," (presentation, *IxDa Interaction 17*, New York City, February 6, 2017).

4. Robert J. Moore and Raphael Arar, *Conversational UX Design: A Practitioner's Guide to the Natural Conversation Framework* (New York: Association for Computing Machinery, 2019); Michael McTear, Zoraida Callejas, David Griol, *The Conversational Interface: Talking to Smart Devices* (Zurich: Springer, 2016); Prakash M. Nadkarni, Lucila Ohno-Machado, Wendy W. Chapman, "Natural Language Processing: An Introduction," *Journal of the American Medical Informatics Association*, 18, no. 5 (September 2011): 544–51, https://doi.org/10.1136/amiajnl-2011-000464.

5. Karen Kaushansky, "Designing the Future, with Voice," (presentation, Front Conference, Zurich, August 30–31, 2018).

6. Matthew Griffin, "Woebot, the World's First AI Counselor, Manages 2 Million Conversations a Week," *Fanatical Futurist*, February 5, 2019, https://www.fanaticalfuturist.com/2019/02/woebot-the-worlds-first-ai-counsellor-manages-2-million-conversations-a-week/;

Dieter Bohn, "Amazon Says 100 Million Alexa Devices Have Been Sold—What's Next?" *Verge*, January 4, 2019, https://www.theverge.com/2019/1/4/18168565/amazon-alexa-devices-how-many-sold-number-100-million-dave-limp.

7. Cade Metz, "Riding Out Quarantine With a Chatbot Friend: 'I Feel Very Connected,'" *New York Times*, June 16, 2020, https://www.nytimes.com/2020/06/16/technology/chatbots-quarantine-coronavirus.html.

8. Ibid.

9. Ibid.

10. Adam S. Miner, Liliana Laranjo, and A. Baki Kocaballi, "Chatbots in the fight against the COVID-19 pandemic." *npj Digital Med.* 3, no. 65 (2020), https://doi.org/10.1038/s41746-020-0280-0.

11. Clifford Nass and Scott Brave, *Wired for Speech: How Voice Activates and Advances the Human–Computer Relationship* (Cambridge, MA: MIT Press, 2005).

12. Ibid. Nass and Brave.

13. Paul Pangaro, "Conversation Is More Than Interaction," (presentation, *IxDa Interaction 17*, New York City, February 6, 2017).

14. Paul Pangaro, personal interview with author, April 16, 2020.

15. Joseph Weizenbaum, "ELIZA—a Computer Program for the Study of Natural Language Communication between Man and Machine," *Commun. ACM* 9, no. 1 (January 1966): 36–45, DOI:https://doi-org.prox.lib.ncsu.edu/10.1145/365153.365168; Joseph Weizenbaum, "Computer Power and Human Reason" (New York: W. H. Freeman, 1976).

16. Paul Pangaro, "Conversation is More Than Interaction," (presentation, *IxDa Interaction 17*, New York City, February 2017).

17. Kent Bye, interview with Rao Kambhampati, "The Landscape of AI," *Voice of AI*, podcast, January 4, 2018, http://voicesofai.com/1-the-landscape-of-artificial-intelligence-with-rao-kambhampati/.

18. Ibid. Kambhampati; Robinson Meyer, "Even Early Focus Groups Hated Clippy," *Atlantic*, June 23, 2015, https://www.theatlantic.com/technology/archive/2015/06/clippy-the-microsoft-office-assistant-is-the-patriarchys-fault/396653/; Abigail Cain, "The Life and Death of Microsoft Clippy, the Paper Clip the World Loved to Hate," *Visual Culture*, 2017, https://www.artsy.net/article/artsyeditorial-life-death-microsoft-clippy-paper-clip-loved-hate; see also Samantha Cole, "Clippy's Designer Wants to Know Who Got Clippy Pregnant," *Vice*, April 26, 2017, https://www.vice.com/en/article/xy-j55a/microsoft-clippy-creator-interview-kevin-atteberry.

19. Sietsma, interview.

20. Steph Hay, "AI + Emotion" (presentation, AIGA Conference, Pasadena, CA, April 5, 2019).

21. Bye, interview with Kambhampati.

22. Weizenbaum, "ELIZA."

23. "Vienna Biennale for Change 2019," Process.studio, March 9, 2020, https://process.studio/works/uncanny-values/.

24. Sidney Fussell, "Alexa Wants to Know How You're Feeling Today," *Atlantic*, October 12, 2018, https://www.theatlantic.com/technology/archive/2018/10/alexa-emotion-detection-ai-surveillance/572884/.

25. Lisa Feldman Barrett, et. al., "Emotional expressions reconsidered: Challenges to Inferring Emotion from Human Facial Movements," *Psychological Science in the Public Interest* 20 (2019): 1–68, https://doi.org/10.1177/1529100619832930; Lisa Feldman Barrett, "Are Emotions Natural Kinds?" *Perspectives on Psychological Science* 1, no. 1 (March 2006): 28–58, https://doi.org/10.1111/j.1745-6916.2006.00003.x; Tim Lewis, "AI Can Read Your Emotions. Should It," *Guardian*, Aug 17, 2019, https://www.theguardian.com/technology/2019/aug/17/emotion-ai-artificial-intelligence-mood-realeyes-amazon-facebook-emotient.

26. Sherry Turkle, *Reclaiming Conversation: The Power of Talk in a Digital Age* (London: Penguin, 2016).

27. Yuval Noah Harari, *21 Lessons for the 21st Century* (New York: Random House, 2019).

28. Kate Darling, "'Who's Johnny?' Anthropomorphic Framing in Human-Robot Interaction, Integration, and Policy" in *Robot Ethics 2.0*, eds. Patrick Lin, Keith Abney, Ryan Jenkins (Oxford: Oxford University Press, 2017).

29. J. C. R. Licklider, "Man-Computer Symbiosis," *IRE Transactions on Human Factors in Electronics*, HFE-1 (March 1960): 4–11.

30. Nicky Case, "How To Become A Centaur," *Journal of Design and Science*, January 8, 2018, https://jods.mitpress.mit.edu/pub/issue3-case https://doi.org/10.21428/61b2215c.

31. Umer Farooq and Jonathan Grudin, "Human-computer Integration" *Interactions* 23, no. 6 (2016): 26–32; see also Florian Floyd Mueller, et.al., "Next Steps for Human-Computer Integration," in *Proceedings of the 2020 CHI Conference on Human Factors in Computing Systems* (New York: Association for Computing Machinery), 1–15, https://doi.org/10.1145/3313831.3376242.

32. Patrick Hebron, personal interview with author, February 13, 2020.

33. Darling, "Who's Johnny?"

34. John Zimmerman, personal interview with author, February 4, 2020.

35. Pattie Maes, personal interview with author, May 7, 2020.

36. Pattie Maes, "Technology Day 2018: AI and Your Health," (presentation, MIT Technology Day Symposium, Cambridge, MA, June 9, 2018).

37. Nataliya Kos'myna and Pattie Maes, "AttentivU: An EEG-Based Closed-Loop Biofeedback System for Real-Time Monitoring and Improvement of Engagement for Personalized Learning," *Sensors* 19, no. 23 (2019): 5200, https://www.researchgate.net/publication/337585925_AttentivU_An_EEG-Based_Closed-Loop_Biofeedback_System_for_Real-Time_Monitoring_and_Improvement_of_Engagement_for_Personalized_Learning.

38. Judith Amores, et al., "BioEssence: A Wearable Olfactory Display that Monitors Cardio-respiratory Information to Support Mental Wellbeing," in *Proceedings of the International Conference of IEEE Engineering in Medicine and Biology Society* (Honolulu, HI: EMBC, 2018). Note: The device can address other symptoms. See https://www.media.mit.edu/projects/bioessence/overview/.

39. Lynn Neary, "Stories Of GPS Directions Gone Wrong," *Talk of the Nation*, NPR, August 12, 2009, https://www.npr.org/templates/story/story.php?storyId=111809897; Timothy Hoff, "Deskilling and Adaptation Among Primary Care Physicians Using Two Work Innovations," *Health Care Management Review* 36, no. 4 (June 2011): 338–48; Tim Harford, "Crash: How Computers Are Setting Us Up for Disaster," *Guardian*, Oct 11, 2016, https://www.theguardian.com/technology/2016/oct/11/crash-how-computers-are-setting-us-up-disaster.

40. Ben Shneiderman, "Human-Centered Artificial Intelligence: Reliable, Safe & Trustworthy," *International Journal of Human–Computer Interaction* 36, no. 6 (2020): 495–504.

41. Harari, *21 Lessons for the 21st Century*.

42. Pattie Maes, personal interview with author, May 7, 2020.

43. Jessica In, "NORAA [Machinic Doodles]," Jessicain.net, accessed March 11, 2020, https://www.jessicain.net/pagesnoraa.

44. Pattie Maes, "AI and Your Health" (presentation, *MIT Technology Day Symposium*, Cambridge, MA, June 9, 2018).

45. Sarah Gold, personal interview with author, June 8, 2020.

46. Sietsma, interview.

47. Kate Crawford "Seeing Like an AI" (presentation, *MoMA R&D Salon 24 AI-Artificial Imperfection*, New York, April 3rd, 2018).

48. Beatriz Colomina and Mark Wigley, *Are We Human? Notes on an Archaeology of Design* (Zurich: Lars Müller, 2017).

49. Erin Friess, "The Sword of Data: Does Human-Centered Design Fulfill Its Rhetorical Responsibility?" *Design Issues* 26, no. 3 (2010): 40–50; Richard Buchanan, "Design Research and the New Learning," *Design Issues* 17, no. 4 (2001): 3–23.

50. For more discussion of symbiotic relationships, see Florian Floyd Mueller, et al., "Next Steps for Human-Computer Integration," in *Proceedings of the 2020 CHI Conference on Human Factors in Computing Systems* (New York: Association for Computing Machinery, 2020), 1–15, https://doi.org/10.1145/3313831.3376242.

51. Anastasiia Raina, personal interview with author, April 7, 2020.

52. See Laura Forlano, "Decentering the Human in the Design of Collaborative Cities," *Design Issues* 32, no. 3 (2016): 42–54.

53. Carl DiSalvo and Jonathan Lukens, "Nonanthropocentrism and the Nonhuman in Design: Possibilities for Designing New Forms of Engagement with and through Technology," in *Social Butterfly to Engaged Citizen: Urban Informatics, Social Media, Ubiquitous Computing, and Mobile Technology to Support Citizen Engagement*, eds. Marcus Foth, et al. (Cambridge, MA: MIT Press, 2011).

54. Anab Jain, "More-Than-Human Centred Design" (presentation, IxDa Interactions 18 Conference, February 8, 2018); see also the work of Anne Galloway, Donna Harroway, Sarah Whatmore, Dorian Sagan, Alex Taylor, Beatriz Colomina, Mark Wigley, and N. Katherine Hayles.

55. Danny Hillis, "The Enlightenment Is Dead, Long Live the Entanglement," *Journal of Design and Science* (2016); see also Jodi Forlizzi, "The Product Ecology: Understanding Social Product Use and Supporting Design Culture," *International Journal of Design* 2, no. 1 (2008).

CHAPTER THREE: PREDICT THE WAY

1. Joanna Peña-Bickley, "Design 2020: Ingenuity in the Key of Industry" (presentation, InVision DesignTalks: Future of UX Design, May 7, 2019), https://www.youtube.com/watch?v=93Fw30tTNiE.

2. For an interesting related discussion around points of possible bias in both the supervised and unsupervised machine learning process, see Anja Bechmann and Geoffrey C. Bowker, "Unsupervised by Any Other Name: Hidden Layers of Knowledge Production in Artificial Intelligence on Social Media," *Big Data and Society* 6, no. 1 (January–June 2019).

3. Kate Crawford and Trevor Paglen, "Excavating AI: The Politics of Training Sets for Machine Learning" (The AI Now Institute, NYU, September 19, 2019); see Cathy O'Neil, *Weapons of Math Destruction* (New York: Broadway Books, 2017); Safiya Noble, *Algorithms of Oppression* (New York: NYU Press, 2018).

4. Bechmann and Bowker, "Unsupervised"; Geoffrey C. Bowker and Susan Leigh Star, *Sorting Things Out: Classification and Its Consequences* (Cambridge, MA: MIT Press, 2000).

5. Crawford and Paglen, "Excavating AI."

6. See Wei Dong, Richard Socher, Li-Jia Li, Kai Li, and Li Fei-Fei, "ImageNet: A Large-scale Hierarchical Image Database," in *Proceedings of 2009 IEEE Conference on Computer Vision and Pattern Recognition* (Miami, FL: IEEE, 2009), 248–55, doi: 10.1109/CVPR.2009.5206848.

7. Kate Crawford "Seeing Like an AI" (presentation, *MoMA R&D Salon 24 AI-Artificial Imperfection*, New York, April 3, 2018).

8. Ibid.

9. Ibid.

10. Joy Adowaa Buolamwini, "Gender Shades: Intersectional Phenotypic and Demographic Evaluation of Face Data-sets and Gender Classifiers" (PhD diss., Massachusetts Institute of Technology, 2017).

11. Zach Blas, "Face Cages," zachblas.info, February 2018, https://zachblas.info/works/face-cages/.

12. Buolamwini, "Gender shades." Jeff Larson, Julia Angwin, and Terry Parris Jr., "How Machines Learn to Be Racist," *ProPublica*, October 19, 2016, https://www.propublica.org/article/breaking-the-black-box-how-machines-learn-to-be-racist; Maria Garcia, "Racist in the Machine: The Disturbing Implications of Algorithmic Bias," *World Policy Journal*, 33, no. 4 (2016): 111–17.

13. Kashmir Hill, "Wrongfully Accused by an Algorithm," *New York Times*, June 24, 2020, https://www.nytimes.com/2020/06/24/technology/facial-recognition-arrest.html.

14. Paul Mozur, "In Hong Kong Protest, Faces Become Weapons," *New York Times*, July 26, 2019, https://www.nytimes.com/2019/07/26/technology/hong-kong-protests-facial-recognition-surveillance.html.

15. Karen Hao, "The Two-year Fight to Stop Amazon from Selling Face Recognition to the Police," *MIT Tech Review*, June 12, 2020, https://www.technologyreview.com/2020/06/12/1003482/amazon-stopped-selling-police-face-recognition-fight/; Kat Kaye, "IBM, Microsoft, and Amazon's Face Recognition Bans Don't Go Far Enough," *Fast Company*, June 13, 2020, https://www.fastcompany.com/90516450/ibm-microsoft-and-amazons-face-recognition-bans-dont-go-far-enough.

16. Noah Manskar and Nicolas Vega, "Amazon's New Gadget Lets You Pay with the Palm of Your Hand," *NY Post*, September 29, 2020, https://nypost.com/2020/09/29/amazon-unveils-supermarket-palm-reader-to-lower-checkout-times.

17. Shoshana Amielle Magnet, *When Biometrics Fail* (Durham, NC: Duke University Press, 2011).

18. Meredith Whittaker, et. al., "Disability, Bias, and AI," AI Now Institute at NYU, November 2019, https://ainowinstitute.org/disabilitybiasai-2019.pdf.

19. Fernanda Viégas & Martin Wattenberg, "Advancing Human/AI Interaction" (presentation, *MoMA R&D Salon 24 AI-Artificial Imperfection*, New York, April 3, 2018); see also https://pair.withgoogle.com/.

20. See "Everyday Ethics for Artificial Intelligence," IBM, accessed March 10, 2020, https://www.ibm.com/design/ai/ethics/.

21 World Economic Forum, "The Global Gender Gap Report" (Genebra: World Economic Forum, 2018).

22. Sarah Myers West, Meredith Whittaker, and Kate Crawford, "Discriminating Systems: Gender, Race and Power in AI," *AI Now Institute*, April 2019, https://ainowinstitute.org/.

23. *Design Census* 2019, AIGA, April 2019, https://design-census.org/.

24. Arun Shastri, "Diverse Teams Build Better AI. Here's Why," *Forbes*, July 1, 2020, https://www.forbes.com/sites/arunshastri/2020/07/01/diverse-teams-build-better-ai-heres-why/#49b44db777b3; Alina Tugend, "Exposing the Bias Embedded in Tech," *New York Times*, June 17, 2019, https://www.nytimes.com/2019/06/17/business/artificial-intelligence-bias-tech.html; Carol Smith, "Intentionally Ethical AI Experiences," *Journal of Usability Studies* 14, no. 4 (2019).

25. Kate Crawford, "Artificial Intelligence's White Guy Problem," *New York Times*, June 25, 2016, https://www.nytimes.com/2016/06/26/opinion/sunday/artificial-intelligences-white-guy-problem.html.

26. Sarah Gold, personal interview with author, June 8, 2020.

27. Caroline Sinders, "AI is More Than Math: Using Design to Confront Bias" (presentation, AIGA Design Conference, Pasadena,CA, April 5, 2019).

28. Charlotte Webb, "Designing the feminist internet" (filmed Nov 2018 in Barcelona, Spain. TEDxBarcelonaWomen video, 19:15), https://www.youtube.com/watch?v=ulzBioEgcHI.

29. Caroline Sinders, "We Need a New Approach to Designing for AI, and Human Rights Should Be at the Center," *AIGA Eye on Design*, March 9, 2020, https://eyeondesign.aiga.org/we-need-a-new-approach-to-designing-for-ai-and-human-rights-should-be-at-the-center/; see also Andrew Smart, et al., "Responsible Innovation for Machine Learning: Toward a Framework for Internal Algorithmic Audits," (presentation, ACM Conference on Fairness, Accountability, and Transparency, Barcelona, January 28, 2020); see also Timnit Gebru, et al., "Datasheets for Datasets," *arXiv preprint arXiv:1803.09010* (2018).

30. Adam Cutler, "AI-Day" (presentation, IBM AI-Day, Auckland, New Zealand, September 18, 2019), https://www.youtube.com/watch?v=ku0l2E4tNTU; see also IBM's *Everyday Ethics for Artificial Intelligence*, https://www.ibm.com/watson/assets/duo/pdf/everydayethics.pdf and Apple's new privacy labels around data use for their apps, Brian X. Chen "Apple Announces New Privacy Features," *New York Times*, June 23, 2020, https://www.nytimes.com/2020/06/23/technology/apple-announces-new-privacy-features.html.

31. Sheena Leek, Isabelle Szmigin, and Emily Baker, "Consumer Confusion and Front of Pack (FoP) Nutritional Labels," *Journal of Customer Behaviour* 14 (2015): 49–61, 10.1362/147539215X14267608004087; Christina Roberto and Neha Khandpu, "Improving the Design of Nutrition Labels to Promote Healthier Food Choices and Reasonable Portion Sizes," *International Journal of Obesity* 38 (2014), https://doi.org/10.1038/ijo.2014.86.

32. Alex Fefegha, "Why We Built an Interactive Tool to Help You Ace AI Basics," *Medium: The Comuzi Journal*, June 11, 2018, https://medium.com/thoughts-and-reflections/why-we-built-an-interactive-tool-to-help-you-ace-ai-basics-e5fda034163d.

33. Charlotte Webb, *Feminist Internet*, accessed June 9, 2020, https://feministinternet.com/projects/.

34. Mimi Onụoha, What Is Missing Is Still There" (presentation, Kikk Festival, Namur, Belgium, November 1, 2019).

35. Diana J. Nucera (Mother Cyborg), accessed April 8, 2019, http://www.mothercyborg.com/.

36. Sarah Gold, personal interview with author, June 8, 2020.

37. Rose Eveleth, "Crime: Can You Sue An Algorithm," *Flash Forward*, podcast, August 27, 2019, https://www.flashforwardpod.com/2019/08/27/crime-bot-court/.

38. O'Neil, *Weapons of Mass Destruction*.

39. Rumman Chowdhury, personal interview with author. February 28, 2020.

40. Ibid.

41. See Mac Hill's research "Visualizing Uncertainty: Developing an Experiential Language for Uncertainty in Data Journalism" (North Carolina State University, Thesis, May 9, 2018), https://college.design.ncsu.edu/thefinally/pdf/Hill-Final-Project.pdf.

42. Sauvik Das and Adam Kramer, "Self-Censorship on Facebook" (Paper International AAAI Conference on Web and Social Media, North America, June 9, 2013), https://www.aaai.org/ocs/index.php/ICWSM/ICWSM13/paper/view/6093.

43. Bruce Schneier, "We're Banning Facial Recognition. We're Missing the Point." *New York Times*, January 20, 2020, https://www.nytimes.com/2020/01/20/opinion/facial-recognition-ban-privacy.html.

44. Glenn Greenwald, "Why Privacy Matters" (filmed October 2014 in Rio de Janeiro, Brazil. TEDGlobal video, 20:30), https://www.ted.com/talks/glenn_greenwald_why_privacy_matters.

45. Ibid; see also Shoshana Zuboff's discussion of the need for privacy in "The Right to Sanctuary," in *The Age of Surveillance Capitalism* (New York: Public Affairs, 2019): 475–92.

46. Heather Dewey–Hagborg Ph.D., "Heather Dewey–Hagborg PhD: Bio-hacker," tellart.com, accessed May 11, 2020, https://www.tellart.com/projects/designnonfiction/.

47. Pattie Maes, personal interview with author, May 7, 2020.

48. Ibid.

49. Nicholas Confessore, "Cambridge Analytica and Facebook: The Scandal and the Fallout So Far," *New York Times*, April 4, 2018, https://www.nytimes.com/2018/04/04/us/politics/cambridge-analytica-scandal-fallout.html.

50. Issie Lapowsky, "One Man's Obsessive Fight to Reclaim His Cambridge Analytica Data," *Wired*, Jan 25, 2019, https://www.wired.com/story/one-mans-obsessive-fight-to-reclaim-his-cambridge-analytica-data/.

51. Lee-Sean Huang, "David Carroll on Data Rights," *Design Future Now*, AIGA, podcast, March 18, 2020, https://anchor.fm/designfuturenow/episodes/David-Carroll-on-Data-Rights-ebk5d3.

52. See New York Times Privacy Project Series, accessed August 10, 2020, https://www.nytimes.com/series/new-york-times-privacy-project; Ted Knutson, "Data Privacy High Concern For Consumers But Many Not Taking Steps To Protect Themselves," *Forbes*, July 29, 2020, https://www.forbes.com/sites/tedknutson/2020/07/29/data-privacy-high-concern-for-consumers-but-many-not-taking-steps-to-protect-themselves/#66ddbd181346.

53. Amanda Lee, "China's Social Credit System Stops the Sale of Over 26 Million Plane and Train Tickets: Statistics from State Planner Show Growing Reach of Beijing's New Social Credit System," *South China Morning Post*, accessed April 19, 2019, https://search-proquest-com.prox.lib.ncsu.edu/docview/2216757835/46DE035803AB4197PQ/3?accountid=12725.

54. Bruce Schneier, "We're Banning Facial Recognition. We're Missing the Point," *New York Times*, January 20, 2020, https://www.nytimes.com/2020/01/20/opinion/facial-recognition-ban-privacy.html.

55. Shoshana Zuboff, "The Age of Surveillance Capitalism," (presentation, Institute of Art and Ideas, London, November 18, 2019).

56. Shoshana Zuboff, *The Age of Surveillance Capitalism* (New York: Public Affairs, 2019).

57. Shoshana Zuboff, "The Age of Surveillance Capitalism." (presentation, The Institute of Art and Ideas, London, Nov 18, 2019).

58. Douglas Rushkoff, *Team Human* (New York: Norton, 2019).

59. The term "dark patterns" was coined by Harry Brignull. See Harry Brignull, Dark Patterns, accessed August 5, 2020, https://darkpatterns.org/.

60. Lilly Smith, "Why You Can't Escape Dark Patterns," *Fast Company*, February 7, 2020, https://www.fastcompany.com/90452333/why-you-still-cant-escape-dark-patterns.

61. Sarah Gold, "Trust and Digital Rights in Learned Systems" (presentation, Google PAIR UX Symposium, Zürich, July 10, 2018).

62. Ibid.

63. ProjectsbyIf.com, accessed June 5, 2020, https://www.projectsbyif.com/; see also Vitaly Friedman, "Privacy UX: Privacy-Aware Design Framework," *Smashing Magazine*, April 25, 2019, https://www.smashingmagazine.com/2019/04/privacy-ux-aware-design-framework/.

64. Guido Noto La Diega and Ian Walden, "Contracting for the 'Internet of Things': Looking into the Nest" (legal studies research paper, no. 219/2016, Queen Mary University of London School of Law, February 1, 2016), https://ssrn.com/abstract=2725913.

65. Ibid.

66. "Kagi," Artefact Group, accessed July 31, 2020, https://www.artefactgroup.com/case-studies/kagi/; see also Liz Stinson, "Can We Trust Digital Assistants to Keep Our Data Private?" *AIGA Eye on Design*, July 1, 2020, https://eyeondesign.aiga.org/can-we-trust-digital-assistants-to-keep-our-data-private/.

67. Anupam Das, et al., "Personalized Privacy Assistants for the Internet of Things," *IEEE Pervasive Computing Magazine: Securing the IoT*, April 2018, https://www.privacyassistant.org/media/publications/IEEE_magazine_2018.pdf.

68. Charlotte Jee, "A New US Bill Would Ban the Police Use of Facial Recognition," *MIT Technology Review*, June 26, 2020, https://www.technologyreview.com/2020/06/26/1004500/a-new-us-bill-would-ban-the-police-use-of-facial-recognition; Sherrod Brown, "Privacy Isn't a Right You Can Click Away," *Wired*, June 29, 2020, https://www.wired.com/story/privacy-isnt-a-right-you-can-click-away/.

69. Ibid.

70. Dr. Rumman Chowdhury, interview by Jeff Frick, Accenture Technology Vision Launch, February 7, 2019, https://www.youtube.com/watch?v=t_wbjmMVNxU.

MIMI ỌNỤỌHA, "WHAT IS MISSING IS STILL THERE"

1. Geoffrey Bowker and Susan Leigh Star, *Sorting Things Out: Classification and Its Consequences* (Boston: MIT Press, 1999).

2. Mimi Ọnụọha, "The Library of Missing Datasets," 2016, https://mimionuoha.com/the-library-of-missing-datasets.

KATE CRAWFORD AND VLADAN JOLER, "ANATOMY OF AN AI SYSTEM"

1. Jorge Luis Borges, "On Exactitude in Science," in *Collected Fictions*, trans. Andrew Hurley (New York: Penguin, 1999), 325.

2. Jean Francois Lyotard, "Presenting the Unpresentable: The Sublime," *Artforum*, April 1982.

3. Yves Citton, *The Ecology of Attention* (Cambridge, UK: Polity, 2017); Shoshana Zuboff, "Big Other: Surveillance Capitalism and the Prospects of an Information Civilization," *Journal of Information Technology* 30, no. 1 (March 1, 2015): 75–89.

4. Alex Hern, "Royal Free Breached UK Data Law in 1.6m Patient Deal with Google's DeepMind," *Guardian*, July 3, 2017, http://www.theguardian.com/technology/2017/jul/03/google-deepmind-16m-patient-royal-free-deal-data-protection-act.

5. Kate Crawford and Vladan Joler, "Anatomy of an AI System: The Amazon Echo As An Anatomical Map of Human Labor, Data and Planetary Resources," AI Now Institute and Share Lab, September 7, 2018, https://anatomyof.ai.

CHAPTER FOUR:
WHO'S AFRAID OF MACHINE LEARNING?

1. See research by Joy Buolamwini, Algorithmic Justice League, accessed June, 2020, https://www.ajl.org/.

2. O'Neil, *Weapons of Math Destruction*.

3. Ethem Alpaydin, *Machine Learning* (Cambridge, MA: MIT Press, 2016), 117.

4. Ibid, 112.

5. Chin-Yuan Fan, Pei-Shu Fan, Te-Yi Chan, Shu-Hao Chang, "Using Hybrid Data Mining and Machine Learning Clustering Analysis to Predict the Turnover Rate for Technology Professionals," E*xpert Systems with Applications* 39, no. 10 (2012): 8844–51.

6. Karen Hao, "The Rare Form of Machine Learning That Can Spot Hackers Who Have Already Broken In," *MIT Technology Review*, November 16, 2018; see also Steven Melendez, "This Security Company Based Its Tech On The Human Immune System," *Wired*, August 8, 2016, https://www.fastcompany.com/3062095/this-security-company-based-its-tech-on-the-human-immune-system.

7. David Silver, et. al., "AlphaZero: Shedding New Light on the Grand Games of Chess, Shogi and Go," DeepMind blog, December 6, 2018, https://deepmind.com/blog/alphazero-shedding-new-light-grand-games-chess-shogi-and-go/.

8. Pedro Domingos, *The Master Algorithm: How the Quest for the Ultimate Learning Machine Will Remake Our World* (New York: Basic Books, 2015); see also Karen Hao, "We Analyzed 16,625 Papers to Figure Out Where AI is Headed Next," *MIT Technology Review*, January 25, 2019, https://www.technologyreview.com/s/612768/we-analyzed-16625-papers-to-figure-out-where-ai-is-headed-next/.

9. Will Knight, "Facebook's New Poker-playing AI Could Wreck the Online Poker Industry—So It's Not Being Released," *MIT Technology Review*, July 11, 2019, https://www.technologyreview.com/s/613943/facebooks-new-poker-playing-ai-could-wreck-the-online-poker-industryso-its-not-being; see also Tom Simonite, "AI Sumo Wrestlers Could Make Future Robots More Nimble," *Wired*, October 11, 2017, https://www.wired.com/story/ai-sumo-wrestlers-could-make-future-robots-more-nimble.

10. Matt Simon, "How Supercomputers Can Fix Our Wildfire Problem," *Wired*, November 29, 2018, https://www.wired.com/story/how-supercomputers-can-help-fix-our-wildfire-problem.

11. Sean Captain, "Here's How To Avoid More Self-Driving Car Deaths, Says Uber's Former AI Chief," *Fast Company*, March 20, 2018, https://www.fastcompany.com/40547165/ubers-former-head-of-ai-heres-how-to-avoid-more-accidents.

12. Alpaydin, *Machine Learning*, 136.

13. Ibid.

14. Dawn Chan, "The AI That Has Nothing to Learn From Humans," *Atlantic*, October 20, 2017, https://www.theatlantic.com/technology/archive/2017/10/alphago-zero-the-ai-that-taught-itself-go/543450/; see also David Silver, et al., "A General Reinforcement Learning Algorithm That Masters Chess, Shogi, and Go Through Self-play," *Science* 362, no. 6419 (December, 2018): 1140–44, https://science.sciencemag.org/content/362/6419/1140.abstract.

15. Karen Hao, "The Rare Form."

16. M. I. Jordan and T. M. Mitchell, "Machine Learning: Trends, Perspectives, and Prospects," *Science* 349, no. 6245 (July 2017): 258, https://science-sciencemag-org.prox.lib.ncsu.edu/content/349/6245/255.

17. Jason Tanz, "Soon We Won't Program Computers, We'll Train Them Like Dogs," *Wired*, May 17, 2016, https://www.wired.com/2016/05/the-end-of-code.

18. Anastasiia Raina "Microbial Cosmologies" (presentation, *Illuminating the Non-Representable*, University of Bergen, Norway, October 2020).

CONCLUSION:
THE FUTURE: EXCITING BUT FRAUGHT

1. Patrick Hebron, personal interview with author, February 13, 2019; see also Sharif Shameem's tool Debuild, accessed November, 2020, https://debuild.co/.

2. Silka Sietsma, "The Future of Design in a Digital-Physical World," Adobe XD Ideas (blog), May 21, 2019, https://xd.adobe.com/ideas/principles/emerging-technology/the-future-of-design-in-a-digital-physical-world.

3. Hebron, interview.

4. Matt Jones, "Centaurs or Butlers? Designing for Human Relationships with Non-Human Intelligences" (presentation, CogX, London, June 2018), https://www.youtube.com/watch?v=gMPbEvtRaEw&feature=emb_logo.

5. Peter Godfrey-Smith, *Other Minds: The Octopus, the Sea, and the Deep Origins of Consciousness* (New York: Farrar, Straus and Giroux, 2016); see Peter Wohlleben, *The Hidden Life of Trees* (Vancouver: Greystone, 2016); see also Kate Darling, *The New Breed: What Our History with Animals Reveals about our Future with Robots* (New York: Henry Holt, 2021).

6. Karl Gerstner, *Designing Programmes* (Zurich: Niggli, 1964).

7. Janelle Shane, "The Danger of AI is Weirder Than You Think," (filmed April 2019 in Vancouver. TED video, 10:28), https://www.ted.com/talks/janelle_shane_the_danger_of_ai_is_weirder_than_you_think.

8. David Ha, "Reinforcement Learning for Improving Agent Design" *Artificial Life* 25 (2019): 352–65, https://arxiv.org/abs/1810.03779.

9. Hebron, interview.

10. Janelle Shane, *You Look Like a Thing and I Love You* (New York: Little Brown, 2019).

11. Molly Wright Steenson, personal interview with author, May 26, 2020.

Image Credits

Front cover, chapter one, chapter two, chapter three, chapter four, conclusion: illustrations by Keetra Dean Dixon

Fig. 1 courtesy of Stephanie Yee

Fig. 2 courtesy of Harrison Lyman

Fig. 3 courtesy of Saqib Shaikh, © Microsoft

Fig. 4 courtesy of John Zimmerman

Fig. 5 courtesy of Rachael Paine

Fig. 7, 11 courtesy of Philip van Allen

Fig. 8 courtesy of Woebot Health

Fig. 9 courtesy of Janelle Shane

Fig. 10 courtesy of Sougwen Chung, Scilicet LLC

Fig. 12, Fig. 13, Fig. 14, Fig. 49 courtesy of Anastasiia Raina

Fig. 15 courtesy of Tellart

Fig. 16 courtesy of Eugenia Kuyda

Fig. 17 courtesy of Josh Clark

Fig. 19 Unknown author, public domain, via Wikimedia Commons

Fig. 20 courtesy of Process Studio (Martin Grödl, Moritz Resl), www.process.studio

Fig. 21 courtesy of Jessye Holmgren-Sidell

Fig. 22 courtesy of Lift Conference, Creative Commons Attribution-ShareAlike 2.5 Switzerland License

Fig. 23, 24, 25 courtesy of Pattie Maes

Fig. 26 courtesy of Jessica In

Fig. 27 courtesy of Sharif Shameem

Fig. 28, 45 courtesy of Artefact

Fig. 29 courtesy of Jasia Reichardt, © Cybernetic Serendipity, 1968

Fig. 30 courtesy of Paul Pangaro, CC Attribution 4.0 International

Fig. 31, 32 courtesy of Superflux

Fig. 33 courtesy of Stephanie Yee and Tony Chu

Fig. 34 courtesy of Timnit Gebru

Fig. 35 Face Cages: Zach Blas, *Face Cage 1*, endurance performance with Zach Blas, 2015, courtesy of the artist; Zach Blas, *Face Cage 2*, endurance performance with Elle Mehrmand, 2014, courtesy of the artist; Zach Blas, *Face Cage 3*, endurance performance with micha cárdenas, 2014, courtesy of the artist; Zach Blas, *Face Cage 4*, endurance performance with Paul Mpagi Sepuya, 2016, courtesy of the artist.

Fig. 36, Fig. 44 courtesy of Sarah Gold, © IF

Fig. 37, Fig. 39 courtesy of Alex Fefegha, © Comuzi

Fig. 38 courtesy of Dr. Charlotte Webb

Fig. 40 photography Pavel Ezrohi; Fig. 47 photography Brandon Schulman; both courtesy of Mimi Onuoha

Fig. 41 courtesy of Tanmay Randhavane

Fig. 42 Installation view of *A Becoming Resemblance*, featuring *Probably Chelsea* (2017) by Heather Dewey-Hagborg and Chelsea E. Manning, August 2– September 5, 2017. Photo by Paula Abreu Pita; courtesy of the artists and Fridman Gallery, New York.

Fig. 43 courtesy of Ece Tankal and Carmen Aguilar y Wedge

Fig. 46 courtesy of Eric Rodenbeck, © Stamen Design

Fig. 48 courtesy of Kate Crawford

Special thanks to North Carolina State University Masters of Graphic Design students who contributed work: Ellis Anderson, Shadrick Addy, Matt Babb, Alyssa Buchanan, Hannah Faub, Randa Hadi, Jessye Holmgren-Sidell, Matt Lemmond, Harrison Lyman, Matt Norton, and Krithika Sathyamurthy.

Text Credits

David Carroll, An Interview. Excerpt from interview originally published as Lee-Sean Huang, "David Carroll on Data Rights," *Design Future Now*, AIGA, podcast, March 18, 2020, https://anchor.fm/designfuturenow/episodes/David-Carroll-on-Data-Rights-ebk5d3, reprinted courtesy of Lee-Sean Huang, AIGA.

Mimi Onuoha, "What Is Missing Is Still There," essay originally published in *Nichons-Nous Dans L'Internet* (April 2018), reprinted courtesy of Mimi Onuoha.

Kate Crawford and Vladan Joler, "Anatomy of an AI System," excerpt from essay originally published as Kate Crawford and Vladan Joler, "Anatomy of an AI System: The Amazon Echo As An Anatomical Map of Human Labor, Data and Planetary Resources," AI Now Institute and Share Lab, September 7, 2018, https://anatomyof.ai, reprinted courtesy of Kate Crawford.

Anab Jain, "More than Human-Centered Design," originally published in earlier version (presentation, Interaction 18 IxDA Conference, Seattle, WA, February 8, 2019), reprinted courtesy of Anab Jain.

Special thanks to Paul Pangaro, Anastasiia Raina, and Philip van Allen for contributing essays.

Index